Helion & Company Limited
Unit 8 Amherst Business Centre
Budbrooke Road
Warwick
CV34 5WE
England
Tel. 01926 499 619
Email: info@helion.co.uk
Website: www.helion.co.uk
Twitter: @helionbooks
Visit our blog http://blog.helion.co.uk/

Text © Efim Sandler 2023
Photographs © as individually credited
Colour profiles © David Bocquelet and Tom Cooper 2023
Maps as credited. Maps by George Anderson © Helion & Company 2023

Designed and typeset by Farr out Publications, Wokingham, Berkshire
Cover design Paul Hewitt, Battlefield Design (www.battlefield-design.co.uk)

Every reasonable effort has been made to trace copyright holders and to obtain their permission for the use of copyright material. The author and publisher apologise for any errors or omissions in this work, and would be grateful if notified of any corrections that should be incorporated in future reprints or editions of this book.

ISBN 978-1-804512-14-2

British Library Cataloguing-in-Publication Data
A catalogue record for this book is available from the British Library

All rights reserved. No part of this publication may be reproduced, stored in a retrieval system, or transmitted, in any form, or by any means, electronic, mechanical, photocopying, recording or otherwise, without the express written consent of Helion & Company Limited.

We always welcome receiving book proposals from prospective authors.

CONTENTS

Abbreviations		2
Introduction by the Editor		2
1	Russia and Chechnya – an Historical Overview	3
2	Caucasian Wars of the Nineteenth Century	5
3	Soviet Times – Revolution and Civil War	8
4	German Offensive on Grozny, 1942	12
5	Deportation and Post-War Period	17
6	Arming Chechnya	25
7	Armed Forces of Ichkeria	29
8	November Rain – the First Armoured Assault on Grozny	34
9	Building the Force	40
10	Moving to War	47
11	First Clashes	51
12	The Way to Grozny	55
13	Approaching Grozny	60
14	Moving into the City (30–31 December 1994)	65
Bibliography		73
Notes		75
About the Author		78

MAP OF EUROPE SINCE 1992

Note: In order to simplify the use of this book, all names, locations and geographic designations are as provided in *The Times World Atlas*, or other traditionally accepted major sources of reference, as of the time of described events.

ABBREVIATIONS

AAA	anti-aircraft artillery	MRD	motor-rifle division
APC	armoured personnel carrier	MRR	motor-rifle regiment
BMD	*boyevaya mashina desanta* (airborne infantry fighting vehicle)	MTLB	*mnogotselevoy tygach legky bronirovanny* (multipurpose light armoured towing vehicle)
BMP	*boyevaya mashina pyekhoty* (infantry fighting vehicle)	MVD	Ministry of Internal Affairs of the USSR (former NKVD)
BRDM	*boyevaya razvedyvatelnaya dozomaya mashina* (combat reconnaissance patrol vehicle)	NKVD	People's Commissariat for Internal Affairs of the USSR
BREM	*bronirovannaya remonto-evakuatsionna mashina* (armoured recovery vehicle)	ORB	independent reconnaissance battalion
		ORBAT	order of battle
BTR	*bronyetransportyor* (armoured personnel carrier)	PGM	precision guided munition
BTS	*bronetankoviy tyagach sredny* (medium armoured tractor)	PMP	*Pontonno-mostovoy park* (ponton/bridge park; a type of mobile pontoon-bridge)
DGB	(Chechen) State Security	PON	operational regiment of the Ministry of Internal Affairs (MVD)
DOSAAF	Volunteer Society for Cooperation with the Army, Aviation, and Navy	RDB	Reconnaissance-Diversionary Battalion
FSB	*Federalnaya sluzhba bezopasnosti* (Federal Security Service)	RPG	rocket propelled grenade
		SPA	self-propelled artillery
GAZ	*Gorkovsky Avtomobilnyi Zavod* (Gorky Automobile Factory)	SPAAA	self-propelled anti-aircraft artillery
		SPAAG	self-propelled anti-aircraft gun
GRU	Main Directorate of the General Staff of the Armed Forces of the Russian Federation (formerly: Main Intelligence Directorate; top Russian military intelligence agency)	SPH	self-propelled howitzer
		UAZ	*Ulyanovsky Avtomobilnyi Zavod* (Ulyanovsk Automobile Factory)
		VDV	*Vozdushno-desantnye Voyska* (Airborne Forces)
MANPAD	man-portable air defence (system)	ZSU	*zenitnaya samokhodnaya ustanovka* (self-propelled anti-aircraft mount)
MRB	motor-rifle battalion		

INTRODUCTION BY THE EDITOR

At first glance, it appears that the First Chechen War (also known as the First Chechen Campaign or the First Russian-Chechen War), fought from late 1994 until mid-1996, was quite a simple affair. Apparently, it pitted Chechen separatists against the central government in Moscow. Insiders recall it as being preceded by the Russian military intervention that culminated in the murderous battle on the streets of Grozny in which dozens of Russian tanks ended as burning wreckage. In a romantic version, it was a showdown between the overwhelming, yet decaying might of the Armed Forces of the Russian Federation and courageous and fiercely resisting, Chechen guerrilla, fought against the backdrop of an almost universal opposition to the conflict by the Russian public – and with mute consent of the West.

To a certain degree, all of this is correct. However, what appears to be a 'simple' conflict between the strongmen controlling the Chechen Republic of Ichkeria of the early 1990s and the Russian Federation and its Chechen loyalists, was not just a minor war, a mere 'internal affair of the Russian Federation'. It was a conflict dating back to at least the eighteenth century; a conflict between the Chechen resistance to the Russian imperialism that experienced its early culmination in the Caucasian War of the nineteenth century and the deportation of thousands of Chechens to the Middle East. It was a conflict that peaked in additional show-downs between the local population and the Russian – and then the Soviet authorities – that culminated in another deportation of thousands – this time to Siberia – in the 1920s and the 1940s. Still, this was not all: it was also a conflict between the growing power of the circles in charge of the Russian intelligence apparatus striving to assume control over all aspects of public life. This included the organised crime within the territory of the federation and de facto, the organised crime of similar circles in what is colloquially known as 'Chechnya' in Russia and outside alike.

This complexity of reasons and lack of serious studies about the context and backgrounds of this war along with huge gaps in the coverage of combat operations, is why, eventually, we have decided to expand this project: from what was originally aiming to cover 'just' the devastating battle of Grozny – 'officially' fought from 22 December 1994 until 6 March 1995 – now into a military history of the First Chechen War.

Without taking sides and always with care to respect veterans of both sides, Efim Sandler has worked for years to collect their recollections and testimonies along with related documentation and diverse publications. The result is a balanced and detailed study of the coming-into-being of the First Chechen War; a meticulous reconstruction of the involved armed forces, regardless of what party and a simple to follow, military history of this conflict peaking in exclusive, minute-by-minute reconstruction of the Battle for Grozny.

Tom Cooper
Olbendorf, June 2023

1

RUSSIA AND CHECHNYA – AN HISTORICAL OVERVIEW

The first mention in Russian sources of Chechen settlements in the valley north of Terek River, is related to the end of the fifteenth and beginning of the sixteenth century. While mistakenly the inhabitants were attributed to either Circassians, Kumyks or even Tatars. By that time, the appearance of people from the Principality of Moscow was absolutely random.[1] Back in 1545, a war began between the Moscow state and the Kazan Khanate, with the latter supported by the Crimean Khanate. Moreover, after another war broke out between Turkey and Iran in 1548 and significant forces of Crimeans were sent to the Asian theatre of operations. This allowed Moscow to capture Kazan in 1552. The latter circumstance, among other factors, increased the role of Russia in Caucasian affairs. It is no coincidence that already in the autumn of 1552, the first embassy from the North Caucasus arrived in Moscow to ask for protection.

Sixteenth – Eighteenth Centuries

The coordinated actions of the Russian troops and detachments of Circassian and Kabardian princes in 1555–1557 along with the terrible drought that hit the Crimea and the Nogai Horde in 1558, followed by hunger and disease which claimed at least a hundred thousand lives from the Nogai alone, allowed Russia to secure Kazan and Astrakhan. Coming out along the Volga to the shores of the Caspian Sea, Russia not only placed important trade routes under its control, but also received a convenient position for further advance towards the Caucasus. Russia was now directly involved in the affairs of the region adjacent to its new borders.

In 1557, Moscow decided to accept the request of the Kabardian princes, Temryuk Idarov and Tazryut, and provide them with patronage. However, it is important to note that this political move did not constitute the actual annexation of Kabarda to Russia. Furthermore, it should be highlighted that the remaining Kabardian rulers did not perceive themselves as being obligated or bound by this action.

The situation underwent a significant change a few years later when escalating civil unrest posed a challenge for the pro-Russian princes. They found themselves in a difficult position and made a request for military assistance. As a result, they agreed to accept a governor, along with adopting Christianity. In response to this appeal, the first Russian military expedition to the North Caucasus occurred in 1560. Ivan Cheremisinov, appointed as the military chief, was entrusted with the tasks of defeating Tarkovsky Shamkhal, conquering the Tyumen principality, annexing Kabarda, and promoting Christianity in the region. Accompanied by a contingent of shooters, Cossacks, and mobilised residents of Astrakhan, the chief embarked on the campaign.

Eventually Cheremisinov invaded Shamkhal and took Tarkov but could not advance to Kabarda which resulted in the first failure of the Russian military campaign in the North Caucuses. Around the same time, the first Russian settlements appeared on the valley-lands of Lower Terek that belonged to the Kabardian princes loyal to Moscow. The Cossacks from Terk-Sunja Ridge, Ataman Kuzma Chervlyony, Schedrin, Gladkov brothers and Kurdyukov, made an agreement with the Kabardian princes and established settlements of Chervlyonaya, Schedrinskaya, Gladkovskaya and Kurdyukovskaya.

In 1567 (or even earlier), on the Terek Spit, at the confluence of the Sunzha with the Terek, a Russian fortress, Terki, had been constructed. After several military clashes with Turkish troops, the Russian government decided to demolish the Terek fortress. However, in 1588, a new Russian fortress Terki (Terek city) was erected on one of the channels in the Terek delta. This was only possible because a number of Chechen princes had entered into an alliance with the Russian governors against Iran and Turkey.

In the same year, the first Chechen embassy, sent by Shikh-Murza Okutsky, arrived in the capital of Russia, at the court of Tsar Fedor Ioannovich. As a result of the negotiations, the relations of the Russian tsar with Shikh-Murza Okutsky were formalised in writing as being relations of suzerain and vassal. The Russian government informed foreign sovereigns about the entry of *Okoks* (later Nakh lands) into 'Russian citizenship'.

In 1594, Tsar troops, having annexed some mountain princes, made an attempt to conquer Dagestan, but were defeated by an army of representatives from Dagestan, Chechnya and Kabarda. The military events in Dagestan sadly affected the position of Moscow's allies in Chechnya: Shikh-Murza was killed, and the Okotskoe possession was devastated. About 160 survivors fled to the Terek city while some of the Nakh refugees were accepted into the Russian service.

At the beginning of the seventeenth century, the population of some southeastern communities of Chechnya were involved in military enterprises against the royal fortresses on the Terek. The position of other Chechen societies, mainly in the eastern and central parts of the region, was apparently favourable to Russia. During the 'Time of Troubles in Russia' during 1605–1614, not only were Russian-Caucasian ties weakened, but also the ties between the metropolis and the Russian settlements on the Terek.

The political situation in the North Caucasus was again aggravated due to the aggressive claims of the Iranian Shah. Turkey, Crimea and Russia simultaneously began to oppose Iran. In 1635, in the northeastern borders of Chechnya, a Sunzhensky stronghold was set-up (between modern Gudermes and Braguns). In 1639, according to the Iranian-Turkish peace treaty, the spheres of influence in the Caucasus were divided. Thus ended a series of Iranian-Turkish wars that had lasted for over a century. By this time, the positions of all the great powers had strengthened in the North Caucasus, each of them with its supporters and vassals.

In the political life of the North Caucasus during the middle of the seventeenth century, the mountain communities of the Chechens of the Argun Gorge began to play a significant role. This related to the struggle of the Georgian king, Teimuraz, against Iran. Counting on military assistance, Teimuraz decided to conclude an alliance with Moscow in the form of recognition of Russian citizenship. The Argun Gorge occupied an important place in the political plans of Teimuraz and the Russian embassy as it was the most important road in the central part of Chechnya.

King Teimuraz arrived in Moscow in 1657 to personally ask for support in the fight against Iran. Representatives of the mountain Nakhs asked for the same and in the summer of 1658, they swore allegiance to Russia at a solemn ceremony in the Assumption Cathedral of the Kremlin. In the same year, through the mediation of Teimuraz, the rulers of the Chechen possession on the Argun entered into friendly relations with the Russian state.

The Russian-Turkish Peace Treaty of 1700 created new opportunities for influencing events in the region. Dissatisfied with the results of the war, the Ottoman Empire tried to raise the mountain peoples against Russia. In 1704, some Chechen and Kumyk feudal lords intended to conclude an alliance with the Crimean Khan in order to destroy the Russian fortifications on the Terek. At the same time, other princes of Chechnya, the Bragun beks, again recognised in 1706 the 'patronage' of Russia.

Both Russia and Turkey sought to enlist the support of the North-Caucasian people by offering rich gifts to local princes. This policy brought mixed success to both sides until 1718, when the Russian government made a serious mistake. A punitive campaign against Chechnya was organised as some kind of friction occurred between the Terek Cossacks and the highlanders (apparently so insignificant that they were not even mentioned in the documents). Several thousand Don Cossacks sent to the Terek ruined the 'Chechen District'. The attack had negative consequences for Russia and its supporters in the North Caucasus: the mountain princes of Chechnya and Northern Dagestan started a war against the royal fortifications on the Terek, and the political situation in the North Caucasus began to take shape in favour of the Crimean Khanate.

After Russia's victory in 1721 in the Northern War and its access to the Baltic Sea, Peter the Great began preparations for a war to access the Black and Caspian Seas. During the campaign of Peter 'to Persia', it was planned to annex part of the North-Caucasian and Transcaucasian lands to Russia. Sources say almost nothing or very little about the situation in Chechnya during this period. It is only known that around the village of Enderi, the combined forces of the Kumyks and Vainakhs entered the battle with Peter's troops and inflicted great damage on them.

However, having suffered a defeat, the Enderian princes gave the Russian tsar an oath, 'including their Chechens for the first time'.

In the autumn of 1722, Peter the Great founded the Holy Cross fortress on Sulak (the city of Terek was demolished and its entire population, including Chechens, was transferred to a new fortress) and visited the territory of modern Chechnya, where he inspected the villages of the Grebensky Cossacks and examined the Bragun warm waters. In the early 30s of eighteenth century the Iranian-Turkish war began, which also affected Chechnya. Iran supported the Crimean Khan. On his side was the Chechen Prince Aydemir with his militia.

The Russian government, opposing the passage of the Crimeans through the North Caucasus, moved towards the troops from the fortress of the Holy Cross. The Russian Army included Chechen soldiers sent by the Chechen princes Alibek and Alisultan Kazbulatov. However, when the Crimean cavalry defeated the Russian Army and an attempt to enslave the peoples of the North Caucasus began, the Chechens and the same Prince Aydemir, who collaborated with the Crimean Khan, swore allegiance to Russia. During the battle between the Chechens and the Crimean troops, up to 10,000 invaders were killed. The Crimean Khan was forced to abandon further attempts to conquer Chechnya.

Armed conflicts in 1757–1758 began in connection with the campaign against Chechnya approved by Empress Elizabeth in order to 'pacify' the masses and restore not only the authority of Russia, but also the princely power that had been shaken. Thousands of warriors from Andi, Avaria, Kumykia and other regions of Dagestan, came to the aid of the Chechens under religious slogans. In turn, the feudal elites took part in the punitive actions of the tsarist troops.

In 1760, the disputed issues were settled through negotiations and returning of hostages from influential families. In 1768, Turkey declared war on Russia. Even before the declaration of war in the North Caucasus, the Sultan's emissaries appeared with generous gifts and appeals to the highlanders to fight against the 'infidels'. With the beginning of the Russian-Turkish war, the Chechen feudal lord, Alisultan Kazbulatov, made a series of attacks on Russian fortifications along the Terek. Later – in February 1770, after being defeated in one of the battles – he, together with his allies, was forced to resume peaceful relations with the tsarist authorities.

Other Chechen and Bragun princes, Raslanbek Aydemirov and Kudenet Bamatov, responded to the request of the tsarist government and joined the Russian Corps operating in the Kuban.

In 1774, at the village of Naurskaya, on the side of the Crimean troops, a 3,000-strong detachment of Chechens and other highlanders marched against the Russians. The detachment was ambushed and defeated by Russian troops.

The performance of the Chechens on the side of the Khan was explained by their dissatisfaction regarding the construction of new Russian

The military structures of the North Caucasian settlements, so called Vainakh towers. It is believed it was this Ingush architectural idea that influenced the North Caucuses from the fifteenth to the seventeenth centuries. The towers could have been for military, civilian or mixed purposes. This picture of the towers of the Chechen settlement of Khani (modern Ingushetia), constructed circa sixteenth to seventeeth century, was printed on a postcard issued by Stockholm based Granbergs Brefkort company in 1904–14. (Efim Sandler collection)

fortifications along the Terek from Chervlenaya to Mozdok. The Chechens considered the left bank lands to be their own and fought for them until the end of the eighteenth century.

After the victory over Turkey, the Russian Empire continued the construction of fortifications from Mozdok to Azov. As a result, a political union arose between the Chechen villages and Kabarda, who had been equally affected by the seizure of the left bank of the Terek. In the autumn of 1779, a battle took place near the Malka River. The brilliantly equipped mountain militia – Chechens and Kabardians, representatives of noble families and professional horsemen – were defeated by artillery fire. This heavy defeat demoralised Kabarda and Chechnya.

In 1785, a powerful popular movement began in the territory of Chechnya, headed by Imam Mansur. This movement developed under religious Muslim slogans. Mansur declared a 'holy war' – ghazavat – to Russia. The 2,000-strong tsarist detachment sent to suppress the uprising was surrounded by mountaineers and destroyed. The rumour about Mansur's victory spread throughout the Caucasus and representatives of various peoples of the Caucasus began to join the detachments of Mansur. Following this, Mansur made a number of attempts to capture Kizlyar but they were unsuccessful. During this period, the tsarist government had to significantly increase the number of its troops in the Caucasus and conduct several military campaigns before Mansur was captured in 1791 and taken to St. Petersburg. Mansur was sentenced to life imprisonment in the Shlisselburg fortress and died in 1794.

2
CAUCASIAN WARS OF THE NINETEENTH CENTURY

In the very beginning of the nineteenth century, a new Chechen leader evolved – Bei-Bulat Taimiev who remained a problem for tsarist troops for many years. In 1802, armed Chechens led by Bei-Bulat, started to ambush Cossack outposts and during one raid, managed to capture Russian Colonel Delpotzzo (retired) who was in one of the Cossack settlements of Terek River.[1]

Despite the generally peaceful policy of Russia towards the mountain people of the North Caucuses, several 'pacifying' expeditions were held. One example in 1805, was led by General Bulgakov and culminated in the Battle of Khankala Gorge, another by General Glazenkov who led his campaign over the Argun River in 1806.

In the same year, a new Commander of Russian Forces in Caucuses, General Gudovich, gathered elder representatives from 104 settlements and offered them terms for cooperation. Eventually Chechens saw this as a weakness and the raids against Russian outposts and settlements increased. The majority of the raids were organised by Bei-Bulat and despite several expeditions, Russians were not successful against the well-armed and highly mobile Chechen detachments.

In 1812, Russia signed the Peace Treaty with Turkey and in 1813, with Persia; effectively ending the respective wars in favour of the Russian Empire. Following the agreements, Russia became the sole ruler of the Caucuses. Such a situation was not well-received by the local inhabitants, especially as they perceived the raids as the daily business of survival rather than being abnormal. Very soon the situation changed.

In May 1816, a new governor of Caucuses was appointed – General Alexey Ermolov. He was tasked with trying to silence the rebellious peoples of the mountains as soon as possible. Ermolov considered the assignment with a broader approach rather than it being just a military operation. He was convinced that only aggressive and merciless means would bear fruits. Ermolov brutally punished not only the raiders but whole settlements, relocating them from the valley-lands towards the mountains. He banned any kind of negotiations or hostage buyouts. Any attempt to take the hostages resulted in imprisonment or execution, of the relatives or elders of the culprit's native settlement.

The General ordered to reinforce Russian settlements and outposts, increasing fortifications, destroying Chechen settlements that were relatively close, wasting the forests, gardens and fields. Tsar Alexander I was in full support for Ermolov's actions. In June 1817, Ermolov ordered the building of a fortress on the Sunja River. For that purpose, the Commander of 19th Infantry Division, Major-General Delpotzzo, led the detachment of six Grenadier companies, 700 Cossacks and four artillery pieces and reported for the mission of 27 June 1817. Sometime later, Ermolov named the fortress, Groznaya. The construction was completed by October 1818 and the first garrison included nine companies of 16th Jaeger Regiment, 400 Cossacks and six artillery pieces.

Meanwhile, the Russians continued their ruthless offensive that often resulted in the destruction of entire settlements. For attacks on Russian officers or government officials, the local inhabitants were imprisoned or even executed – such cases happened in 1819 with Dadi-Yurt and Gersel-Aul in 1825. In turn, several Chechen uprisings happened in 1821, 1823 and 1826, under command of Bei-Bulat and Abdul-Kadyr, but all were aggressively suppressed by Russians. Bei-Bulat joined the Russian military service in the rank of lieutenant and took part in a campaign against Turkey until he was killed in an act of bloodline revenge by Kumyk Prince, Salat-Girey Eldarov in 1831.

Overall, the policy of General Ermolov did not bring about the expected result and the mountain people were never happy to be loyal to Russia. In 1827, Ermolov was forced to retire and was replaced by Graf Ivan Paskevich. Paskevich changed the tactics from a massive and slow offensive to lightning raids on Chechen strongholds – still Russians were in constant engagements with numerous detachments of mountain people.

In 1828, a new leader was rising – Imam Gazi-Muhammad who was actively promoting Islam as the base for the struggle against Russian colonial policy in the Northern Caucuses. Gazi-Muhammad went from settlement to settlement to promote *muridism* – basically Sufism inspired liberation ideas. His efforts bore fruits and by 1829, he had about 8,000 men and in early 1930, he declared 'holy war', *gazavat*, on Russia and its allies.

In his first attempt to engage a force loyal to Russia, Avar Khanate, was unsuccessful and eventually he lost his entire force

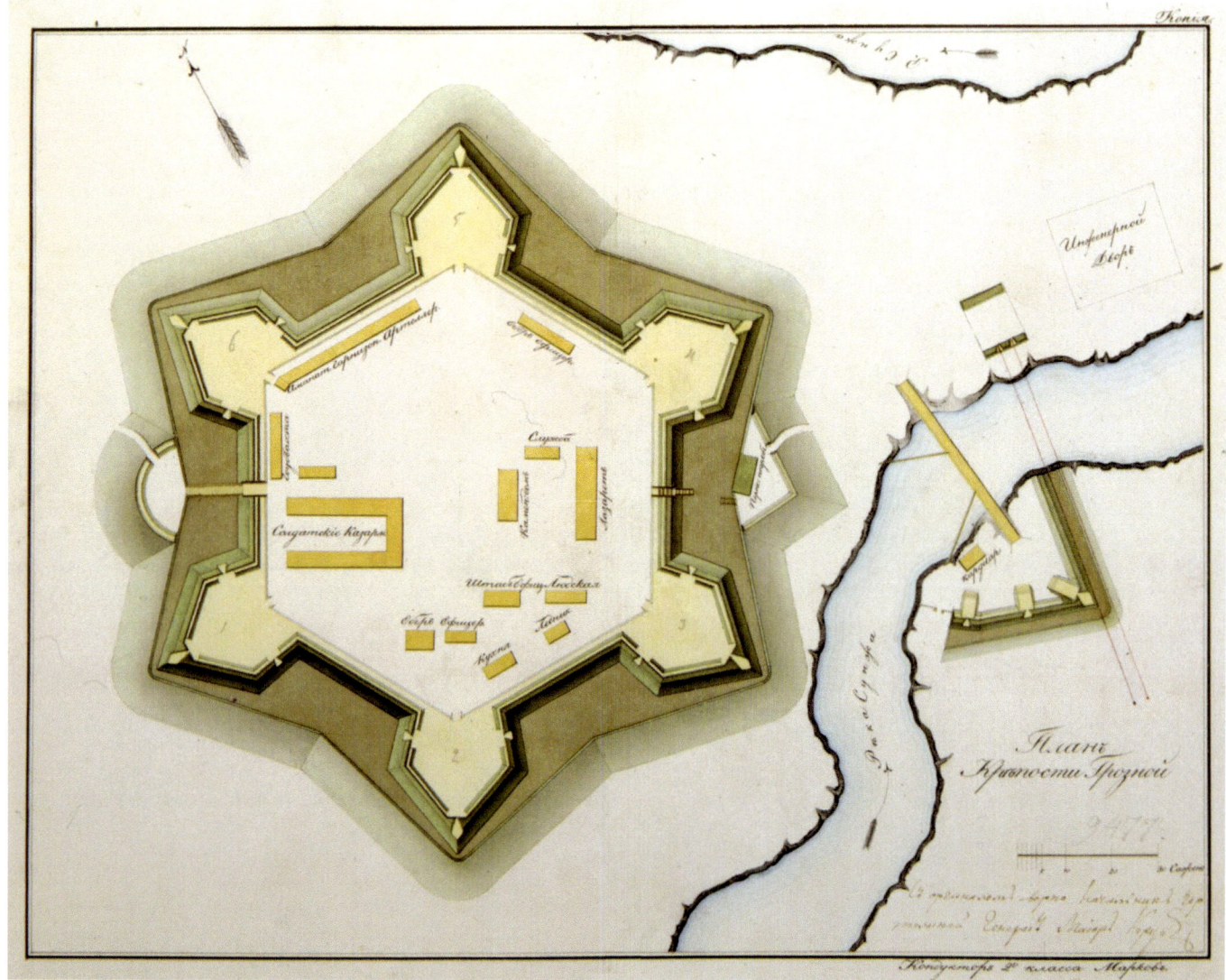

The fortress of Groznaya as constructed on the orders of General Yermolov in 1817–18. The sketch was hand-painted by the artist visiting the fortress circa 1820 and copied by topographic service of Russian Empire Engineering Corps in the early twentieth Century. (via Efim Sandler)

while trying to do so – one part was killed, another part switched sides, while others simply went home. Gazi took this defeat as a starting point and spent the rest of the year establishing a new force and deciding on tactics that would work best for mountain people. The tactic became known as 'dog and flea' – avoiding head-to-head engagements, making lightning hit and run attacks on small groups and garrisons, setting up ambushes and using hardly accessible terrain to hide within. He also mentored his forces not to stick to particular settlements.

The first victory of the newly formed mountain opposition occurred in July 1831 when the commander of the Caucasian Line, General Georgy Emanuel, led an expedition to unblock the Russian fortress of Vnezapnaya and destroy Imam Gazi-Muhammad forces. Moving through the dense forest near Aktash-Aul, a Russian convoy of 2,500 men with 10 artillery pieces, spread over a large distance, was subject to numerous ambushes that resulted in over 400 dead and captured while the General was badly wounded in the chest.

In November 1831, Gazi-Muhammad arranged a very ambitious raid to attack Kizlyar. Only 600 men from the original detachment of about 1,500 reached Dagestan and attacked Kyzlyar. Russians gave a tough fight and the Chechens did not manage to take over the fortifications but overran the town and destroyed it. General Alexey Velyaminov, the loyal supporter of Ermolov, had been appointed as Commander of the Caucuses Line and was tasked with destroying Gazi-Muhammad forces. General Velyaminov once again switched the tactics of Russian forces – the main detachment was deployed towards its objective and while it started to construct the fortifications, small units ran around the objective, both probing the defences and learning the terrain.

After all necessary observations were done, the major offence by numerous small detachments was initiated resulting in a good outcome with low casualties. In 1832, he managed expeditions in Dagestan and Ingushetia destroying over 60 settlements, while Gazi-Muhammad appeared in Chechnya and attacked the settlements of the lords loyal to the Russian Empire.

Slowly but surely, Russian forces took ground and managed to locate Gazi-Muhammad in his native settlement of Gimry. During the assault, Imam Gazi-Muhammad and most of his men were killed. One of the few who survived the Russian onslaught was one of Gazi-Muhammad guards and a close friend called Shamil, still unknown to many. The next leader of the murid movement was Imam Gamzat-Bek who managed to take over the Avar Khanate capital of Khunzakh and executed scores of locals including the Khan's sons.

After the massacre in Khunzakh, Gamzat-Bek became an outlaw as many mountain people wanted him to stand down. Finally in September 1834, he and most of his murids were annihilated by Avar Khan's relative, Khadji-Murat in an act of bloodline revenge.

After the end of the Caucasian Wars in 1864, Groznaya Fortress was renamed Grozny and received the status of a town in 1871. The fortification remained in place with the garrison but all the settlements around were bounded under one municipality. (via Efim Sandler)

In September 1834, Shamil was elected as the new Imam of Dagestan and Chechnya by a people's assembly in the Dagestani settlement of Ashilta. It is important to note that Shamil was mainly known in Dagestan but ironically, his main rival, the leader of the people of Chechnya – Sheikh Tashu-Khaji – did not arrive on time and the young and ambitious Shamil took the opportunity to persuade the assembly members to elect him.

Tashu-Khaji was not happy to learn he was Shamil's subordinate and treated him as an equal ally at the most – their relations remained pretty complex until Tashu's death in 1845. Imam Shamil took the national idea to the next level – he decided to establish a state based on Sharia laws – Imamat. With the help of Turkish, Egyptian and British advisers, Shamil established political and military structures, he introduced taxation and administrative authorities – naibs and mudirs with their teams of officers.

Shamil's vision of legislation was based entirely on Islam and merciless punishments for any deviation. His first step was to tackle the areas loyal to the Russian Empire and he began to take over settlements – often performing public executions. Notably, not everyone (especially in Chechnya) supported the Imamat with its strict laws; historically, Chechens preferred to live their lives within their clans (teips) and many felt well treated under Russian patronage and did not want to become subjects for destruction, either by Shamil or by Russians.

Throughout the next couple of years, Shamil and Tashu-Khaji performed numerous raids against Russian forces and settlements loyal to Russia. In 1837, Russians performed several successful punitive expeditions in Chechnya, Dagestan and Ingushetia under General Karp Fezi and destroyed a number of settlements including one near Mount Akhulgo, blocking the residence of the Imam in Teletl' but they did not take over it.

After several weeks of the blockade, Fazi met with Shamil and the latter gave a promise not to destroy Russian forces or mountain people loyal to Russia. It soon became obvious that the promise of Shamil was worth nothing and an enraged Emperor Nikolai ordered the complete destruction of Shamil through any available means.

In 1839, a large Russian force under General Pavel Grabbe, pushed Shamil forces to the fortress of Akhulgo. The assault lasted for over two months with both sides suffering heavy losses. Finally, the fortress was taken on 22 August 1839 but Shamil and about 30 of his murids, managed to escape. From out of about 3,000 murids and their families, almost none survived. During the assault, Shamil's wife, new-born son and his sister died.

Russian losses were over 2,500 including 500 killed. Grabbe reported the victory to St. Petersburg that considered the fall of the Imamat as an absolute success of Russian military in the North Caucuses. In 1839–40, Russian forces performed several expeditions aimed to disarm locals and trace any loose detachments of murids. Shamil in turn, returned to the tactics of 'dog and flea', ambushing Russian troops in harsh terrain and focusing on the anti-Russian propaganda among Chechens which underlined the feudal essence of the Russian Empire.

In 1840, Shamil moved to Chechnya, started to gather forces and was joined by several warlords – including the killer of Imam

Gamzat-Bek, Khaji-Murat, who had switched sides. The same year, Shamil made several successful actions against Russian forces and declared a new Imamat in the capital at Dargo-Vedeno. The years of 1843–47 was the peak of the influence of Shamil's Imamat as he managed to hold the major powers with no real contender. Meanwhile, a large part of mountainous Dagestan and almost the whole of Chechnya, were under his control – after suffering several painful defeats in 1843 and especially in 1845, the Russians had to pull back.

Within time, the Imamat became a scene of rivalry between Shamil naibs who in turn, focused on personal wealth and corruption. From 1849, Russian forces returned to General Ermolov's strategy of squeezing – they encircled the Imamat with large numbers of troops and slowly advanced, securing the gains with numerous fortifications and garrisons. Russian actions yielded results and starting from 1850, the Imamat began to experience heavy economic difficulties after losing the valley-lands.

In 1851, Shamil lost his most potent commander – Khaji-Murat switched sides again and turned to Russians after 12 years of service for Shamil. In the same year, the Russians suffered the loss of the very successful General Nikolai Sleptsov who had conducted several expeditions with great results and minimal losses. Sleptsov was shot dead during another successful engagement near Gekhi River on 10 December 1851.

In 1853, another Russo-Turkish war (aka Crimean War) started and Shamil hoped that it would cause Russia to release the pressure but eventually, the opposite happened – the Russian Empire committed over 200,000 troops for the Northern Caucuses and in 1856, started a major offensive under General Nikolai Evdokimov. The hunger of 1856–57 that hit the mountain people due to Russian blockages made things worse and Shamil started to lose one commander after another.

In 1856, General Alexandr Baryatinsky had been appointed as new Commander of Separate Caucasian Corps (Russian troops in the Caucuses). He followed Ermolov's strategy but with less aggression and cruelty, giving his opponents a chance to switch sides. In 1858, Shamil's forces suffered a painful loss at the Battle of Achkhoy and in the following year, General Evdokimov took over the Imamat capital of Vedeno, finally cleaning Chechnya and followed Shamil into Dagestan.

On 10 August, General Baryatinsky's troops secured Shamil and about 400 murids in the village of Gunib, and on 25 August 1859, Shamil turned himself over to the Russians. The operations continued mostly in the Black Sea areas and formally, the war was over on 21 May 1864 when Russian forces met in Kba'ade (area of modern Adler). On 26 August 1866, Shamil and two of his sons took an oath of loyalty to the Russian Empire and in 1869, the Emperor, Alexander II, gave permission to release Shamil to perform Hajj to Mecca.

3
SOVIET TIMES – REVOLUTION AND CIVIL WAR

The news about the February Revolution came to Grozny on 28 February 1917 and almost instantly, triggered the activity of various underground groups that started to disarm policemen and set-up the local militias. On 5 March, the Grozny Council of Workers and Soldiers Deputies (aka Grozny Council) was founded with most of the places taken by Social-Democrats and Social-Revolutionists but ironically, headed by the Bolshevik, Nikolai Anisimov. In April – May, the Council was slowly taking over power in Grozny but conversely, the rivalry between the parties started to show, basically mirroring the situation in Petrograd.

In July, the first riots started of the 21st Cossack Regiment and its garrison in Grozny and were only suppressed in August by the arrival of Terk Cossack units who were loyal to the government and set-up a martial law. Trying to disarm the militants, the Cossacks triggered a stronger opposition of Bolsheviks – the workers began to organise in para-military structures and on 24 September, the Red Guard was founded.

On 26 October, the news of the Bolsheviks seizing power in Petrograd reached Grozny and Grozny Council welcomed the transition to the Soviets. On the other hand, the Right-wing parties, Terk Cossacks and Union of Mountain People, did not receive it well, and demanded to disarm the workers militias and the Grozny garrison that had been 'poisoned' by Bolshevik propaganda.

The soldiers of the 111th Regiment located in Grozny, held a different opinion and took the change of powers as licence to do whatever they wanted, which led to anarchy. The situation spiralled out of control in early November when armed confrontation between the 111th Regiment and Chechen Regiment guarding the railway station, led to the death of about 30 horsemen of the Chechen Regiment, including the son of the Chairman of Union of Mountain Peoples. The events led to the cooperation of Terk Cossacks and the Union of Mountain Peoples followed by the establishment of a Terk-Dagestan Provisional Government. On 27 November, the units of the new government with about 1,000 horsemen, took control of Grozny and meeting no opposition (the majority of the Grozny garrison had fled days before), started a wave of murders and looting.

By the end of 1917, the situation in Grozny was very confusing – three parties (Leftist Grozny Council, Cossacks and Chechen National Council) were constantly changing sides. The Chechens who occupied Grozny had to withdraw and were replaced by two regiments of Cossacks who mostly repeated the behaviour of their predecessors – murdering and looting. In December, the confrontation between the Cossacks and Chechens evolved into armed conflict with numerous engagements around Grozny, Gudermes and all over the Sunja River.

The military leadership of the Terk-Dagestan region decided to support the Cossacks and supplied a large number of weapons from depots in the town of Georgievsk. On 26 December, the Commissar of Grozny District of Chechen National Council, Sheikh Deni Arsanov and about 30 of his murids, were killed by Cossacks in Groznenskaya settlement, while trying to negotiate a truce. The murder of Arsanov triggered frantic action from Chechens and on the next day, several Cossack settlements came under siege by murids who also pushed Cossacks from Gudermes, cutting the communications with Grozny.

Under these circumstances, the Grozny Council and Terk Cossacks, formed Grozny District Military Revolutionary Council; this was taken by the Bolsheviks as a chance to reinforce their positions in Grozny. The new Council instantly began to prepare for defensive operations – the town was divided into sectors that hosted armed militias headed by Commissars reporting to Council.

On 1 January 1918, the Chechen settlements of Stary-Yurt and Bamat-Yurt were attacked by Cossack forces from the side of Chervlennaya and Terk Ridge and the Revolutionary Council, from Grozny direction. On the same day, by the order of the Revolutionary Council, all of the Chechen population of Grozny was taken to prison and held as hostages. Despite numerical superiority and extensive usage of artillery, including an armoured train constructed in Grozny, the Cossacks were defeated during the fight near Stary-Yurt and pulled back with heavy losses.

The victorious Chechens immediately turned on the Cossack settlements and the hostilities continued until the truce was negotiated at the end of January. Ironically, after an unsuccessful offensive initiated by the Revolutionary Council, the Bolsheviks quickly reversed allegiance, condemned Cossack leadership and expressed support for common Chechens. Meanwhile, divisions appeared in the Chechen National Council due to the prevailing influence of Islamic spiritual leaders being confronted by a group of Leftist activists, including the future Chechen Bolshevik leader, Aslanbek Sheripov.

At the end of January, Cossack leadership offered the Bolsheviks an opportunity to form an alliance and declare a war against Chechens and Ingush, in turn promised to accept the control of the Soviets. The Bolsheviks did not take the bait as they already coordinated their positions with other socialist parties and did not want to associate themselves with adventurous plans of the Cossacks. In Grozny, the power moved to the Bolsheviks who, by February, ruled in the Grozny Council headed by Nikolai Gikalo.

In March, the 2nd Congress of Terek Peoples formally accepted the Power of the Soviet of People's Commissars, headed by Vladimir Lenin. Terk Oblast was proclaimed as an autonomy in the Russian Federation – the Terk Soviet Republic. In April, Bolsheviks performed a reorganisation of authorities in Grozny and openly started to form the Chechen Red Army, under command of Mikhail Levandovsky.

The declaration of the Power of Soviets in Terek triggered fierce opposition of the Centre and Right-wing factions of the Union of Mountain Peoples that had been forced to relocate to Abkhazia. In April 1918, representatives of the Union met with Turkish leadership in Istanbul and were informed about the intentions to create an independent state in the North Caucuses. The Turks were positive and promised military support against Soviet Russia while the Germans, who were Turkey's allies, remained silent, observing the developing situation.

In May, the Union announced an independent Mountain Republic from the Black Sea in the west to the Caspian in the east. The new republic quickly signed an agreement with Turkey and the latter moved its troops from Baku to Dagestan. Meanwhile the third side – the Cossacks, planned a plot to take power in Terek. On 23 June, the Terk Cossack-Peasant Council was formed in Mozdok, under the leadership of Colonel Georgy Bicherakharov and supported by the 1st Kizlyar-Greben Cossack Regiment.

Shortly afterwards, Bicherakharov's men destroyed local Bolshevik Soviets and disarmed the Red Army units reporting to them – the events became known as the Bicherakharov Uprising. The Red Army deployed additional forces who were defeated on 30 June losing a very important railway hub, the Station of Prokhladnaya. At this point, both sides paused as neither was ready to continue the operations. Bicherakharov did not have enough heavy weapons and had to keep a good portion of his men to guard the settlements against pro-Bolshevik Chechens, while the Red Army in Terk had the same issue with lack of heavy weapons. Additionally, it had lost Mozdok and Prokhladnaya and was cut off from the main forces deployed in Kuban. Despite the numerical superiority of the Red forces in Terk Oblast (25,000 versus 12,000), the Cossacks were better organised and much better trained.

The Bicherakhov forces became active after the British troops arrived in Baku. The first attempt to challenge the Bolsheviks was in Vladikavkaz, which was attacked on the night of 5–6 August by Cossacks led by Colonels Belikov and Sokolov. The fighting lasted 11 days and the attackers were repelled by the Red Army units commanded by Levandovsky but not without the help of Ingush locals who supported the Bolsheviks and arranged several raids against Cossack settlements in the area.

During the fighting in the town, Mikhail Levandovsky practised the tactic of localising the enemy strongholds whilst putting the pressure on them and simultaneous advancing, slowly and carefully, clearing building by building. This tactic worked well for the Red Army and by 18 August, Vladikavkaz was under its total control. At the same time, the situation around Grozny became extremely alarming. Bicherakhov placed an ultimatum on Grozny Council for immediate disarmament and throwing out all Bolsheviks. By then, the Council was almost completely controlled by the latter and issued an ultimatum for Cossacks in Groznenskaya to give up all their weapons.

Eventually, both sides appeared to be ready for the fighting that started on the morning 11 August 1918 and which became known as '100-Day Fights'. During the day, both sides extensively used artillery to hammer enemy positions. Nevertheless, the Cossacks managed to take over several districts and the railway station, blocking Council forces from three directions. Fortunately for the Bolsheviks, they received reinforcements of about 1,500 men from the Chechen Red Army, led by Aslanbek Sharipov which reinforced the positions in the south leaving the corridor for the valley-lands of Chechnya open. In this light, paramount importance was laid on the Goity settlement that took the Bolshevik position and secured the supply routes.

After stabilising the situation in Grozny, the Red forces became active in two additional directions. Pro-Bolshevik Chechens were targeted to sabotage the railways in order to prevent reinforcements for the Cossacks coming from Iran – by night, Chechens were demolishing the tracks and by day, Bichekharov forces were busy rebuilding. In addition, the Bolsheviks sent a team of experienced agitators, headed by Terk People's Council Commissar, Alexander D'yakov, to work with the Sunja Cossacks. The Soviets promised the Cossacks to stop Chechen attacks on the settlements in response for their support against Bichekharov.

The first joint Cossack-Chechen detachment with 300 members was formed on 2 September. In just one week, D'yakov had under his command about 4,000 men, including 200 Chechens and 100 Ossetians. After the Red Army stormed and took over the Cossack settlements of Sleptsovskaya and Mikhailovskaya, the Red Cossack forces numbers mounted to 6–7,000.

However, Bichekharov's misfortunes continued in October when the reinforcements, led by General Mistulov, were blocked in Kizlyar and had to retreat under pressure of fresh Red Army units arriving from Astrakhan. On 29 October, the Red forces in Grozny took over the railway station and in two weeks it was all over. By 14 November 1918, Grozny was in the hands of the Bolsheviks and the Red Army held a parade to mark the victory. The 100-Day Fights was one of the fiercest battles of the Civil War, with dozens of thousands taking part and about 4–5,000 killed.

In early 1919, the 11th Red Army responsible for the southern direction, collapsed under the attack of the Volunteer Army of General Denikin so pulled back towards Astrakhan, exposing the whole North Caucuses frontier. The Commissar of the South, Grigory (Sergo) Ordzhonikidze, tried to improve the situation by setting up the defence line, Vladikavkaz-Grozny, but his efforts were voided by typhus and mass defection in the Red Army.

A unique image of Chechen Islamic leaders (from right to left) – Emir Uzun-Khaji, Imam Nadzhmidin Gotsinsky, Sheikh Siradzhudin-Khaji, Mikhail Khalilov, Daniyal Apashev. Pictured in Temir-Khan-Shura, 1918. (via Efim Sandler)

On the night of 2–3 February, Red Army units left Grozny and moved to Vladikavkaz but were blocked by White and Cossack forces at the Sunja line and fled to the Chechen mountains. This was the end of the Terk Soviet Republic. However, Ordzhonikidze made another move and declared a Mountain Soviet Republic. As usual, Bolshevik propaganda worked well and a large number of locals supported the Bolsheviks. It is believed that about 5–6,000 of Red troops took shelter in the mountains of Chechnya.

Unlike the Bolsheviks, Denikin's command decided not to deal with local authorities, calling them 'aborigine chiefs', acting in a very arrogant manner and very soon, they were subject to extensive sabotage. At the end of February, the White forces of Pavel Shatilov's Division tried to assault the Goity settlement. Chechens proved to be very committed to fighting and repelled the enemy with heavy losses.

In March, Denikin's forces managed to take over several settlements to the west and east of Grozny but as usual, the Chechen and Red Army units put up a hard fight and caused heavy casualties on the attackers. The fighting continued through spring and summer while the Chechen Red Army, led by the former Chairman of Grozny Council, Nikolai Gikalo, started to rebuild itself based in Argun Gorge with its headquarters in Shali.

As a temporary solution, the Bolsheviks made a treaty with the newly formed North-Caucasian Emirate, led by famous the religious activist, Sheikh Uzun-Khaji, known for his anti-Denikin position. In June 1919, Nikolai Gikalo arrived in Vedeno for negotiations with Sheikh and managed not only to get approval for his actions on the territory of the Emirate, but he also became a Commander of 5th Separate Army of Imamate (read Chechen Red Army).

The Army of Emirate started its actions against Denikin's forces in August with the fight for Serzhen-Yurt and again on 11 September, when 5th Army attacked and pushed the Whites out of Vozdvizhenskaya. The fighting continued and on the night 22–23 December, Red forces under Gikalo's command, started an uprising in Grozny that eventually failed and triggered massive executions of Bolshevik supporters. On the other side, Denikin's forces were defeated by the Red Army just some 300km from Moscow. The massive advance of the Soviets and rapid collapse of the Whites and Cossacks, made it possible for Gikalo to re-establish the Chechen Red Army and on 24 January 1920, it took responsibility of all separate detachments in Terk Oblast.

On 17 March, Gikalo's units took over Grozny with almost no opposition – Denikin's army literally dissolved. On 24 March, elements of the 11th Red Army reached Grozny and joined Gikalo' forces. A delegation sent from Sheikh Uzun-Khaji arrived shortly to negotiate the future of 'Red-Emirate relations' only to receive unnegotiable conditions from the Bolsheviks to formally accept Soviet power. Ironically, the 72-year-old Sheikh Uzun-Khaji died before this news could reach him and the Emirate was no more.

In the spring of 1920, the anti-Soviet movement in the North Caucasus unfolded immediately after the liberation of the region from the White Guard troops. By September 1920, the first reports of the Chechen's hostile attitude towards the regime, started arriving in Moscow. One of the reasons for hostility was the impossibility of a rapid improvement in the economic situation of the mountain peoples of the North Caucasus, due to the extreme complexity of the economic and political situation of Soviet Russia itself. Despite the endowment of the highlanders with land at the expense of the Cossack population in the autumn 1920 and the allocation of significant funds for the development of the economy, the difficulties had not been overcome.

A significant role in the instigation of the anti-Soviet movement was played by people who had previously actively supported the White Guards; former officers of the tsarist army and kulaks, now became members of the revolutionary committees of Chechnya, Ingushetia and Dagestan. Muslim religion also played a major role in the negative development of the situation. The almost universal illiteracy of the mountain peoples created favourable ground for religiosity, reaching almost to fanaticism and the appearance of numerous holy sheikhs and mullahs.

An important part in the development of banditry in the region was played by the cult of weapons among the mountain peoples. After the end of the Civil War, the number of weapons found in the hands of the population, could not be counted because, 'every single boy had his own weapons'.

Nazhmutdin Gotsinsky was the leader of the anti-Soviet movement in the North Caucasus in the first half 1920s and he led the uprising which spread over Dagestan in 1920–21. In May 1923, in the Chechen villages of Makazhoy and Khimoy, a meeting of the of bandit groups' leaders was held under the chairmanship of Gotsinsky. The agenda focused on the hostilities against the Soviet regime, preparation of the mass uprising and acquiring military equipment from abroad.

In Dagestan at the end 1923, the detachments under the control of Gotsinsky committed 68 raids. In Chechnya during July – October 1923, gangs committed 107 raids, including six on military depots and four on railway facilities. Under the current conditions, the South-East OGPG affiliate undertook a number of operations aimed at the forceful elimination of the anti-Soviet gang leaders. In April 1924, the Chechen department of the OGPU carried out a successful operation in Grozny, a result of which one of the active Gotsinsky supporters, Sheikh Ali Mitaev, was arrested.

On 6–12 May, Dagestan OGPU launched an operation to locate Gotsinsky but the latter managed to escape capture losing several of his close men. On 31 July 1925, Soviet leadership decided to inflict a crushing blow to rebels by carrying out large scale operations to disarm local populations and attempt the 'removal of the bandit element' throughout the North Caucasus.

The plan of the operation was based on a sudden rapid disarmament of the population of the mountainous regions with the use of maximum repression in order to force the population to hand over the hiding gang leaders. For this, the territory of Chechnya was divided into seven districts, within each, a certain military group and an operational group of the OGPU would operate. The main centres of banditry were identified as the Zumsoevsky community (six settlements) and the Keloi-Dai District of the Shatoevsky District, where Nazhmutdin Gotsinsky, Sheikh Emin Ansaltinsky and Atabi Shamilev were allegedly located.

The Group of the Red Army consisted of 6,183 people, armed with 137 heavy and 102 light machine guns, 14 mountain and 10 light guns. The amount of OGPU troops was decided on the basis of an order from the authorised representative of the OGPU dated 8 August 1925 – a total of 341 people. To prevent the escape of gangs into the territory of Georgia, detachments of the Caucasian Labour Army and the Transcaucasian CheKa, numbering 230 people, set blocking positions on the border.

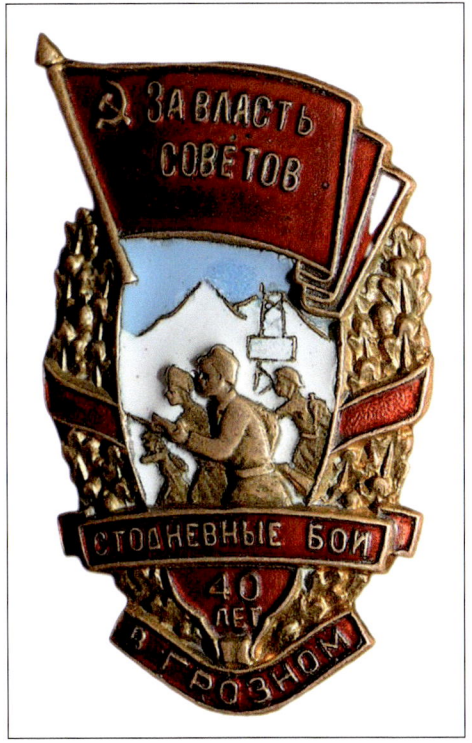

The badge issued in 1958 to commemorate the 40th anniversary of 100-Day Fights in Grozny. (Efim Sandler collection)

The operation to disarm Chechnya began on 25 August 1925 simultaneously in all mountain regions. On 29 August 1925, another operational-military group was created under the leadership of the head of the Chechen department of the OGPU, Sergey Mironov, whose task was to capture Gotsinsky and his associate Atabi Shamilev, who had hidden in remote mountainous areas.

On 5 September 1925, in a cave near the villages of Khimoy and Khakmada, Nazhmutdin Gotsinsky and Sheikh Dzhavatkhan of Zumsoy, who offered no resistance, were arrested. Gotsinsky was urgently taken to Rostov-on-Don, where on 15 October 1925 he was sentenced to death and executed.

During the operation, 25,299 rifles, 4,319 revolvers, one Lewis machine gun, two English machine guns, one Maxim machine gun, one mountain gun and about 75,000 rounds of ammunition were seized. Of the 242 disarmed settlements, 101 villages refused to voluntarily surrender their weapons and were subjected to a 10-minute artillery and machine gun fire. 16 settlements, where the most prominent gang leaders were hiding, were subject to aerial bombardment by 16kg bombs that resulted in the destruction of 119 houses. During the shelling, six civilians were killed and 30 wounded. During the operation 309 'hostile elements were removed', from them 105 executed. Soviet losses were five men killed and eight wounded.[1]

4
GERMAN OFFENSIVE ON GROZNY, 1942

On 22 June 1941, the Germans launched Operation Barbarossa and invaded the Soviet Union. With the rapid advance through 1941 and the failure in the Battle of Moscow, German command decided to review the plans for 1942 and focus the main effort on the southern direction with the goal of taking over the oil hubs of Baku and Grozny. During the first half of 1942, the Red Army continued to pull back and by August, the Germans were close to the borders of Chechen-Ingush Republic. According to the plan, German forces of Army Group A, commanded by Field Marshal Wilhelm List, were to advance in three directions: over the Black Sea shoreline, towards Novorossiysk, Sukhumi and Batumi; over the North Caucuses towards Kutaisi and Sukhumi; and the major offensive towards Grozny, Makhachkala and Baku with flanking of Tbilisi and Ordzhonikidze.

The Grozny direction was under responsibility of General Paul von Kleist having under his command, 1st Panzer Army with three armour and three infantry divisions. Almost immediately after the launch of German advance, Soviet forces started to prepare an echeloned defensive line around Grozny. The North (Caucasian) Group of Red Army, commanded by General Ivan Maslennikov, included 37th Army in the Nalchik direction and 9th Army in the Malgobek direction.

By the end of August, the city was prepared for the war with very complex set of fortifications including over 1,000 strongholds, 28km of anti-tank ditches filled with water and oil, 9km of ramps with oiled soaked straw and large areas of soil filled with a mixture of gas, kerosene and raw oil. In Grozny itself, there were 70km of trenches, 4km of anti-tank fortifications, 5km of barricades and 16km of barbed wire fences. In addition, there were 800 anti-tank hedgehogs, 399 hardened concrete covers and about 250 strongholds.

On the night of 30 August, the combat group of the 3rd Panzer Division, based on the 394th Motorised Infantry Regiment and reinforced by sapper companies, with the help of the 906th Assault Boat Detachment, including powerful artillery support, crossed to the southern bank of the river near the village of Ishcherskaya which had been captured the day before. The area of the crossing and the bridgehead captured by the Germans, were immediately subjected to raids by Soviet bombers and attack aircraft. All attempts by the enemy to transport the tanks were repulsed by the actions of aviation and the fire of artillery.

Following this, counterattacks by units of the 389th Infantry Division (Lieutenant-Colonel Serafim Krasnovsky), as well as advanced units of the 417th Infantry Division, advanced from the reserve of the Northern Group of Forces (Colonel Semyon Storozhilov) and the Germans were driven back to their original positions. The relatively small forces of the XL Panzer Corps involved in the operation, showed that the crossing of the Terek at Ishcherskaya was demonstrative and distracting. The information obtained by military intelligence confirmed that the main blow would be delivered in the defence zone of the XI Guards Rifle Corps deployed in the centre of the formations of the 9th Army (the neighbour on the left being the 151st Rifle Division, the neighbour on the right was the 389th Rifle Division while the 176th Rifle Division was in the second army echelon). This covered the most promising direction for the enemy's offensive on Malgobek-Grozny.

German Panzerkampfwagen III Ausf J/M tanks, probably of 5th SS Viking Division preparing to cross Terek River in September 1942. (Photo by Gerhard Gronefeld)

Shortly before the attack, the scouts of the 9th Guards Rifle Brigade of the XI Guards Rifle Corps captured an Oberst Lieutenant, commander of a sapper battalion of the 370th Infantry Division. Together with other officers of the Division, he participated in the reconnaissance of the Terek River when they were attacked by a Soviet reconnaissance group that secretly crossed the front line. During the battle, the commander of the 666th Infantry Regiment, Major Knut, and several officers were killed and the Oberst Lieutenant was captured.

During interrogation, the prisoner testified that the 370th Infantry and 3rd Tank Divisions were concentrated in the Mozdok area and that there were many crossing facilities, artillery and mortars. According to the prisoner, an offensive in this direction should be expected from day to day. It also became known that in the defence zone of the XI Guards Rifle Corps, Germans deployed the main forces of the 13th Panzer and 111th Infantry Divisions. However, the information that the 11th Guards were occupying positions in the direction of the main attack of the 1st Panzer Army was not properly assessed.

As a result, the command of the 9th Army did not use the time to radically strengthen the defensive line of the Guards Corps. The 111th Infantry Division of the Wehrmacht began crossing the Terek south of Mozdok near the village of Predmostny on the night of 2 September. 8th Guards Rifle Brigade (Lieutenant-Colonel Pavel Krasovsky) was holding the defensive positions on the southern bank of the river. The Germans hoped to cross unnoticed on inflatable boats in complete silence, without artillery preparation and to transfer the Company of the 50th Infantry Regiment with the first wave of landings. However, the boats were discovered and met with dense rifle and machine gun fire. Following this, the Germans called a powerful artillery strike aimed at the previously reconnoitred targets.

A few hours later in the morning, the crossing of the Terek began near the village of Kizlyarsky (Kizlyar), on the right flank of the defence of the 9th Guards Rifle Brigade (Lieutenant-Colonel Andrey Vlasov), the left neighbour of the 8th Guards Rifle Brigade. The battalion of the 668th Infantry Regiment of the 370th Infantry Division, which was crossing the river in large and small inflatable boats and motor assault boats, put up with stubborn resistance. Whilst at the bridgehead of Predmostny, the Germans managed to land and clear the coastal strip in just 20 minutes, whereas in the Kizlyarsky area it took almost 1.5 hours.

On 3 September, expanding the bridgehead at Predmostnoye, significant forces were already operating – the 117th Infantry Regiment was in full force with units of the 50th Infantry Regiment and some other formations of the 111th Infantry Division, supported by a battery of the 191st Brigade of assault guns and a battalion of tank regiment of the 23rd Tank Division.

At Kizlyarsky, an infantry battalion of the 370th Infantry Division and a group of tanks from the 3rd Panzer Division, crossed to the right bank. The accumulation of enemy troops on the right bank of the Terek was facilitated by constant powerful artillery support from the opposite bank with fire adjustment by artillery observers in infantry combat formations. On 4 September, during a raid by Soviet aircraft, as a result of direct bombings, the bridge near Predmostnoye was seriously damaged, and traffic was restored only a day later.

The raids on the bridges south of Mozdok went on almost continuously from 18:00, 4 September to 03:30, 5 September. The intensity of the bombing attacks on temporary bridges across the Terek was such that the sappers barely had time to restore the destroyed crossings. As a result of a Soviet air raid on the night of 5 September, almost all vehicles located there were damaged in the crossing area and two anti-aircraft guns were hit. On the evening of 4 September and on the night of 5 September, the advanced command posts of both infantry divisions were also subjected to air strikes, which led to a partial loss of contact with the troops.

Although Pe-2 and Douglas Boston bombers of the 219th Bomber Aviation Division (Colonel Ivan Batygin), bombed the bridge areas and quite successfully dropping bombs from a height of 3 – 3,500 metres, they suffered considerable losses. According to German reports about the Terek crossings on 2 September, six bombers and cover fighters were shot down. From the fire of anti-aircraft artillery and as a result of attacks by a few fighters of the 3rd Group of the 52nd Fighter Squadron (III/JG.52), two bombers were lost on 6 September, the next day the same number.

The small number of German fighter aircraft was compensated by the effectiveness of the latest Messerschmitt models – Bf109G – which were controlled by experienced pilots. At night, the female pilots of the 588th Night Bomber Aviation Regiment (Major Evdokiya Bershanskaya) of the 218th Night Bomber Aviation Division, armed with U-2 light-engine aircraft, went on a mission. Despite the small bomb load, which did not exceed 200kg, night bombers, flying one at a time with an interval of 3–4 minutes, acted on targets from a height of 800–1,000m. Due to the continuity of the impact, this had a very distracting effect on the German troops.

For the first time, the Red Army Air Force had succeeded in influencing the operational situation. By acting in close cooperation and in the interests of Ground Forces, Soviet pilots demonstrated the true power of strike aviation, fettering the actions of the advancing enemy. Never before, not in 1941 nor in the first half of 1942, had the Germans experienced Soviet aviation in such extent and intensity.

On 4 September, Germans launched an offensive from the Predmostnoye in a southern direction. Using numerical superiority over 8th Guards Rifle Brigade who had suffered losses in previous days, the Germans overcame the defences and reached the positions of the 62nd Naval Rifle Brigade of Colonel Serafim Kudinov, who had arrived the day before from the Western Front, was deployed in the second echelon of the XI Guards Rifle Corps. The commander of the Corps, Major-General Ivan Rosly, from his observation post, saw how up to 10 tanks with machine gunners on the armour, broke through to the location of the command post of the 62nd Brigade.

General Rosly ordered the neighbouring 9th Guards Rifle Brigade to immediately strike at the flank of the advancing enemy and then counter-attack with the forces of the 62nd Naval Brigade, supported by the 249th Separate Tank Battalion. Here, it experienced its first battle (CO Captain Ivan Marunyak, died on September 5, 1942) with 30 M3l Stuart and M3s Lee tanks, as well as the 47th Anti-Tank Artillery Battalion.[1] By joint well-coordinated efforts, the situation was stabilised by the evening.

On 6 September, the enemy made another attempt to break into the defences of the Red Army on the right bank of the Terek. Germans managed to force the 62nd Naval Rifle Brigade back, and formed a corridor up to 2,000 metres wide, right at the junction of the 8th Guards and the 9th Guards Rifle Brigades, and thus to advance for 5–7km to the south. However, the Germans failed to expand the breakthrough zone. Decisive counterattacks of the Soviet troops, including 10th Guards Rifle Brigade (Colonel Sergey Bushev), with strong fire support of 98th Guards Artillery Regiment and 152mm howitzers of 68th Army Artillery Regiment, deprived the enemy of a real prospect of success.

Taking advantage of the favourable situation, the command of the 9th Army decided to launch a counter-attack in order to restore the position of its troops, completely clearing the southern bank of the Terek from the enemy. On the morning of 7 September, the XI Guards Rifle Corps, reinforced by a rifle regiment from the 417th Rifle Division, cooperated with the tank group and concentrated 7km north of Malgobek – the 52nd Tank Brigade (Colonel Ivan Chernov) and the 75th Separate Tank Battalion (Major Alexey Shutov), went on the offensive.

The tank group was relatively numerous, numbering 76 tanks but as both units were introduced into battle for the first time, most of the personnel had no combat experience. In addition, the tank brigade had to perform a combat mission immediately after a long transition in the face of strong enemy opposition from the air. The beginning of the counter-attack was extremely unsuccessful. The commander of the 52nd Tank Brigade launched 30 heavy KV and medium T-34 tanks into the attack on a narrow sector of the front, hoping to suppress the enemy's fire system, break through his defences and lead the infantry – the 8th Guards Rifle Brigade and the 62nd Naval Rifle Brigade – to the crossings near the Predmostnoye and Kizlyarsky. This would solve the key task of regaining control over the right bank of the Terek.

On the eve of the offensive, no reconnaissance was carried out, the possibilities of the enemy's anti-tank defence were not assessed and the interaction with infantry and support artillery was not worked out. Preparation for solving a complex combat mission was actually limited to a brief half-hour reconnaissance of the area, which was carried out by Colonel Chernov with the commanders of tank and motorised rifle battalions and the commanders of individual brigade companies, roughly specifying the direction of the formation.

As a result of many hours of battle, 16 tanks (14 T-34 and two KVs) were lost, 120 people died or went missing. Only three heavy KV tanks and up to 20 light T-60 tanks remained combat-ready in the brigade (light tanks did not participate in the attack and had no losses). 'For his inability to organise and ensure combat operations, as well as his indecisiveness', Colonel Chernov was removed from command of the brigade and put on trial. His deputy, Major Vladimir Filippov, became the brigade commander.

The Germans stepped up their offensive against the XI Guards Rifle Corps. On 11 September, two infantry regiments of the 370th Infantry Division, supported by tanks of the 4th Panzer Regiment (13th Panzer Division) attacked along the southern bank of the Terek. The day before, 10 September, enemy tankers had lost their commander – the commander of 4th Panzer Regiment, Colonel Herbert Olbrich, was killed – but this did not weaken their offensive impulse. Under pressure from superior forces, units of the 9th Guards Rifle Brigade had to retreat 4–5km.

The next day, continuously building up forces on the southern bank of the Terek and overcoming the resistance of the 9th Guards Rifle Brigade, the 52nd Naval Rifle Brigade, as well as a tank group (52nd Tank Brigade, 75th and 249th Separate Tank Battalions), the Germans launched an attack on the village of Malgobek (Lower Malgobek), which was captured on 12 September.

The further offensive of the enemy in the east was held back by units of the 176th Rifle Division (Colonel Ivan Rubanyuk) along with the elements of the XI Guards Rifle Corps. The 151st Rifle Division (Colonel Vladimir Kolesnikov), which was transferred to the 37th Army, also tried to counteract the Germans in the west and south-west direction. Nevertheless, on the morning of 13 September and advancing with heavy fighting, the 13th Panzer Division captured the village of Nizhny Kurp (Nizhnyaya Kurpatskaya), reaching the rear of the 151st Rifle Division, which was turning its front along the Terek, to the east.

In the battles to the west and south of the village of Malgobek, parts of the Division suffered heavy losses. The 581st Rifle Regiment lost 70 percent of its personnel and one of the battalions was completely destroyed. From the 626th Rifle Regiment, a battalion defending in the Nizhny Kurp area was dispersed. In the evening, the enemy captured the village of Upper Kurp. By the end of the day on 14 September, as a result of a decisive counter-attack by the strike group of the 37th Army (assembled from units of the 151st and 275th Rifle Divisions, as well as units of the 60th Rifle Brigade and the 113th Rifle Regiment of the NKVD), the village was again captured by Soviet troops. Further advance of the enemy between the 37th and 9th Armies was thus suspended.

Along with the strike group of the 37th Army which achieved some success, two strike groups were assembled and a counteroffensive of the 9th Army was prepared in order to decisively turn the tide at the Mozdok bridgehead. The counteroffensive did not bring much triumph. As a result of three days of fierce fighting, both sides suffered large losses, while for Soviet troops they were much more significant. In some areas, units of the XI Guards Rifle Corps managed to advance 4–5km, and in the area of the 275th Rifle Division of the 37th Army, some 5–8km.

The situation at the Mozdok area had not actually changed. By that time, the bridgehead already occupied a significant area – up to 40km wide and up to 20km deep. On 19 September, having repelled a series of counterattacks by the 9th Army, the enemy again went on the offensive, firmly intending to change the course of events. The 13th Panzer Division, deployed on the left front of the bridgehead, struck at the combat formations of the 151st Rifle Division and advanced westward towards Kuyan. To the south, from the area of the village of Nizhny Kurp, the 370th Infantry Division, supported by a tank group, advanced on Planepskoye.

The 151st Rifle Division, bled dry in the battles of the previous days, was forced to withdraw to the left (western) bank of the Terek, taking up defence there with separate centres of resistance with a front to the east. As a result, the left flank of its neighbour on the right, the 275th Rifle Division, was exposed.

Under the growing pressure of units of German 370th Infantry Division, fearing flank seizure and the enemy reaching the rear, 275th Division also had to retreat to the left bank of the Terek. Continuing the offensive to the west, the Germans overcame the extended defensive formations of the Soviet troops, crossed the river, capturing Maisky and Aleksandrovskaya by 23 September.

The enemy offensive received significant reinforcements after Ewald von Kleist reassigned the 5th SS-Freiwilligen-Division (motorised) 'Wiking' (CO Felix Steiner) to the command of the 1st Panzer Army and there was a hasty transfer from the Tuapse to the Grozny direction. The Division, staffed by Nordic states, along with three motorised infantry regiments, artillery and other support units, consisted of a newly formed tank battalion – SS-Pz.Abt.5 (Commander Johannes-Rudolf Mühlenkamp) with two companies of 17 Pz.Kpfw.III tanks each, one company of 10 Pz.Kpfw.IV, each having HQ section with platoon of light Pz.Kpfw.II Ausf.F. In addition, the Division had an anti-tank battalion, SS-Pz.Jg.Abt.5, with one company of 12 Marder II, 7.62cm Pak36(R) auf Fgst. Pz.Kpfw.II(Sfl.) anti-tank vehicles, and two companies of towed artillery, mostly captured from Red Army.

For active offensive operations in the Grozny direction, a powerful fist was assembled from three tank divisions, a motorised SS Division and two infantry divisions. The direction of the

An ex-Canadian Valentine Mk.VIIA tanks from the 5th Guards Tank Brigade, North Caucasus Front, 1942. (Photo by Max Alpert)

main attack shifted to the east, to the city of Malgobek (Eastern Malgobek). On the night of 24–25 September and in the afternoon of 25 September, the main forces of the SS Division crossed to the southern bank of the Terek and advanced to the first line on the front of the 9th Army. The Division received the order – together with the 111th infantry Division, supported by the StuG Abteilung 191st (Assault Artillery Brigade) and the strike group from the 23rd Panzer Division – to defeat the Soviet troops between Nizhny Kurp and the village of Malgobek, before launching an offensive in a southeast direction towards the village of Sagopshin and the town of Malgobek.

The blocking positions of the western entrance to the Akhan-Churt valley were assigned to the 52nd Tank Brigade of Major Filippov, deployed in the Sagopshin area, replenished after losses in the September battles and included about five heavy tanks KV-1, two to three medium T-34, 13 light T-60 and eight M3l Stuarts. The Brigade was reinforced by the 863rd Anti-Tank Artillery Regiment of Major Fyodor Dolinsky, as well as a combined battalion assembled from Red Army soldiers and commanders of the 57th Rifle Brigade.

In the predawn fog of 28 September and without any artillery preparation, the SS Viking Tank Battalion, reinforced with the infantry of SS Westland Regiment and with more than 40 tanks and anti-tank self-propelled guns, moved to the defensive orders of the Soviet troops. Behind the armoured vehicles at 200–300m, units of the Westland regiment advanced in a foot formation. The calculation was that hiding behind the dense fog and not being exposed to the enemy fire, the attackers would easily and without loss, break into the location of the Soviet troops.

However, the plan for surprise did not come about as around 07:00, the fog cleared and in a matter of minutes, the Germans found themselves among a Soviet defensive line and were instantly hammered with artillery fire, mortars, anti-tank rifles and all types of small arms. In about an hour, German losses mounted to nearly 50 percent of the initial force, with the infantry being cut off from the tanks.

The tanks of the Viking Battalion had to engage Soviet 52nd Brigade from a distance of hundreds of metres where they had no superiority. By the end of the day, Viking Battalion had to retreat to initial positions losing from between 19 to 28 tanks (upon various sources), Soviet losses amounted 10–15 tanks confirmed by both sides. One German Pz.Kpfw.III was recovered and joined the orders of 52nd Brigade.[2]

To strengthen the defence capabilities and prevent the Germans from advancing along the Akhan-Churt valley, the command brought in the 5th Guards Tank Brigade of Colonel Pyotr Shurenkov. Being in the reserve, the Brigade had no losses and had 44 tanks including 40 Mk.III Valentines, three T-34s and one BT-7. The arrival of a fresh unit significantly strengthened the position at the entrance to the Akhan-Churt valley. Until 3 October, the enemy tried to break through the defences of the Soviet troops but did not succeed in moving forward.

Maglobek was defended from the west by the 176th Rifle Division, exhausted by many days of battle and supported by the 62nd Naval Rifle Brigade, as well as the 417th Rifle Division and brigades of the XI Guards Rifle Corps. Northwest of Malgobek, the 59th Rifle Brigade held the defence. The main forces of the 52nd Tank Brigade were transferred directly to the Malgobek area to support the infantry who operated from the fixed positions.

Realising that the front could not be held by available forces, the command of the Transcaucasian Front transferred the 347th

Commander of 52nd Tank Brigade, Major Vladimir Filippov, pictured near Mozdok on 9 September 1942. Major Filippov commanded the Brigade during the fight against 5th SS Division near Sagopshin, on 28 September. (Photo by Yakov Khalip)

and 317th Rifle Divisions to urgently advance to the area of the 9th Army. On 5 October, the forces of 111th Infantry Division with the SS Regiment Germania, supported by the Viking Tank Battalion and the 191st Assault Gun Battalion, as well as units of the SS regiment Norland of 5th Division, moved to Malgobek. The first to reach Malgobek were the assault groups of the Germania SS Regiment. Before the decisive move – closer to noon – the battle formations of the Soviet troops, which by that time had already been pushed to the outskirts of the town, were attacked by a large group of up to 20 Stuka dive bombers from StG 77.

The brunt of the fighting on 7 October fell on the 62nd Naval Rifle Brigade, which along with the participation of units of the 176th Rifle Division and part of the forces of the 256th Rifle Brigade, held back the advance of two regiments of the Viking Division, supported by the forces of its tank battalion. On that day, the Viking Division, the 111th Infantry Division and the 13th Panzer Division Battle Group, who were trying with all their might to build on the success after the capture of Malgobek, managed to advance only 1.5–2.5km.

Using well-prepared defensive positions closely linked to the nature of the terrain, the Soviet troops reduced the enemy's successes to extremely limited results. Most of the enemy attacks were also repulsed on 8–9 October and the Soviet 417th and 347th Rifle Divisions, also involved in active operations, managed to completely hold their positions. The command of the 9th Army made the most of all the forces at its disposal, to support the troops fighting in the Malgobek area.

In addition to the 52nd and 5th Guards Tank Brigades and the 75th and 488th Separate Tank Battalions, the 15th Tank Brigade (Colonel Ivan Kochin) arrived after being staffed from the reserve of the Transcaucasian Front. In total, by 10 October, more than 170 tanks were in the listed tank formations, including seven heavy KVs, 16 medium T-34s, 68 MKIII Valentines, with the rest being light T-50, T-60 and M3ls. Particularly intense battles took place in the following days for the dominant height 701, southeast of Malgobek, which was key in the defence system of the Soviet troops.

With the forces of the 3rd (Finnish) Battalion of the Nordland Regiment and the powerful support of the Viking Divisional artillery, the 111th Infantry Division and the corps artillery of the LII Army Corps, the assault on the height began on 9 October but ended in failure the same day.

Trying to prevent further attacks, from 10 October, the Soviet command organised a series of counterattacks along the entire line of contact in the Malgobek direction. The fighting for height 701 continued until 16 October when the major forces of Finnish Battalion of the Nordland Regiment attacked under cover of darkness and took the exhausted men of Soviet 9th Rifle Brigade by surprise.

By 18 October, both sides in the Malgobek direction were finally exhausted. The counterattacks by the Soviet troops, adhering to the tactics of active defence, in which it was possible to send more and more limited forces, were beaten off by the enemy without much effort. However, the Germans, who suffered serious losses, were unable to organise a successful offensive operation.

One of the reasons for the stabilisation of the front line was the terrain, on which the troops of the 9th Army managed to create insurmountable defensive lines. Chains of hills and uplands, ravines and riverbeds served as a natural basis for creating fairly stable defensive zones. Together with trenches, covered firing positions and artillery positions, the defence was supplemented by engineering structures – minefields, heavy explosive setups, anti-tank ditches, as well as ditches and thatched shafts, flooded and doused with oil. Only at the cost of heavy losses in personnel, weapons and equipment, with inadequate grinding of the offensive potential achieved, did the enemy manage to gnaw through the defences, bumping again and again into new defensive lines. By the end of October, the German offensive on the Grozny direction was finally stopped and never reactivated again.

5
DEPORTATION AND POST-WAR PERIOD

It is thought that the decision to deport Chechens and Ingush was taken by Stalin in connection with the events that took place within the autonomy during the Great Patriotic War. In fact, the following happened; with constant uprisings and anti-Soviet activity, Chechnya did not arrive at peace until 1941 whilst the last major military operation with the mass seizure of weapons, took place in 1940. With the outbreak of war, mobilisation in the Chechen-Ingush autonomy went relatively well for some time and thousands of Chechens and Ingush, mobilised in 1941, went to the front. However, more and more often, the population of the Chechnya tried to avoid this situation and since 1942, deployment in Chechnya has been thwarted. In total, only 28,000 Chechens and Ingush took part in the Second World War.

More concerning for the Kremlin were the renewed uprisings in the territory of the republic. In October 1943, Commissar of State Security, Bogdan Kobulov, sent a note addressed to the People's Commissar of Internal Affairs, Beriya, with an alarming number of deserters. In addition, it was reported that about 2,000–3,000 Chechens were members of anti-Soviet gangs who were active in the mountains killing Soviet officials and NKVD members.

There were also reports of Chechen groups used by the Germans to infiltrate areas in the rear of Soviet troops, sabotaging communication lines. It was very easy to persuade Stalin to take punitive measures to eliminate the threat in such a strategically important area especially after the movement of the war pushed the Germans off the Caucuses. Stalin had never forgotten the amount of trouble that the Chechens caused during his time as Commissar of Nationalities, 1917–1923.

By 02:00 on 23 February 1944, all settlements were cordoned off, ambushes and patrols were set-up, radio broadcasting stations and telephone communications were turned off. At 05:00, the men were called to meetings where they were told the government's decision. Immediately, the participants at the gatherings were disarmed and operational groups were already knocking on the doors of Chechen and Ingush houses. Each operational group, consisting of one operative and two soldiers of the NKVD troops, was supposed to evict four families.

The operational group action pattern was as follows: upon arrival, a search was carried out at the house of the deportees, during which firearms and cold weapons, currency and anti-Soviet literature were confiscated. The head of the family was asked to extradite the members of the detachments created by the Germans and those who helped the Nazis. From 23 to 29 February 1944, 478,479 people were evicted and loaded onto 177 railway trains, including 91,250 Ingush and 387,229 Chechens. Additionally, two days later, over 5,000 men were taken from the mountain settlements that had limited access due to snowstorms.

During the preparation and conduct of the operation, 780 men were killed, 2,016 people among Chechens and Ingush were arrested in connection with anti-Soviet activities. 20,072 firearms were confiscated, including 4,868 rifles, 479 automatic rifles and machine guns. 6,544 locals managed to avoid the deportation and fled to mountains. The lion's share of the deported Chechens and Ingush were sent to Central Asia – about 400,000 to Kazakhstan and about 80,000 to Kyrgyzstan. In parallel, Chechen and Ingush members were demobilised from the Soviet Army and the majority sent for to construction works in the north with no permission to return to their homeland. During the first half of 1944, 710 officers, 1,696 NCOs and 6,488 soldiers were demobilised from frontline units.

On 9 January 1957, the Decree of the Presidium of the Supreme Soviet of the USSR 'On the restoration of the Chechen-Ingush Autonomous Soviet Socialist Republic within the RSFSR', was signed, effectively ending the deportation period. A massive return of Chechens triggered a wave of criminal activity towards non-Chechen inhabitants (mostly Russians) which peaked in riots during 1958 after a Russian youngster was killed by a group of Chechens.

ISU-152 self-propeller artillery of the 'heavy battalion', 392nd Training Tank Regiment (m/u 61652) based in Shali pictured in maintenance and repair area, 1972-74. (Photo via 392 Regiment veterans)

T-62 tanks of 392nd Training Tank Regiment, during the 100km march exercise in Argun Gorge, 1972-74. (Photo via 392 Regiment veterans)

However, there was the welcome arrival of additional working resources which were much-needed after the war. In the late USSR, Checheno-Ingushetia became a deeply peripheral zone. After the discovery of the Siberian oil fields, the significance of the Caucasus for the Soviet economy declined, although oil remained the basis of the economy of the Checheno-Ingush ASSR (Soviet Autonomous Republic). Chechnya remained a predominantly agricultural region with a low level of education and weak prospects.

At the same time, a significant part of the urban population (although a minority) were Russians and representative of other peoples. In total, in 1989 there were 718,000 Chechens in Chechnya, 292,000 Russians and Ukrainians and about 15,000 Armenians; 222,000 Slavs lived in the capital of the Republic of Grozny, making up 56 percent of the population. People of non-Chechen nationality were most often engaged in professional labour and had a higher level of education and prosperity. In addition, many descendants of the Cossacks lived in the villages, especially in the north of Chechnya.

It is worth mentioning the military establishments in the territory of Checheno-Ingushetia in Soviet times. After the war, the Soviet Army started a chain of reorganisations in late 1940s, 1950s and 1960s that affected all units, including those based in the North Caucuses. By 1 September 1949, a newly formed 24th Yevpatoriyan, Red Banner Rifle Division had been relocated to Checheno-Ingush Republic with the headquarters in Grozny. The Division was based on the 3rd Separate Rifle Brigade of Moscow Military District. In 1951–54, the Division was qualified as Mountain-Rifle with respective training and weapons set.

On 1 June 1957, the Division was reassigned to XII Army Corps with a new designation – 42nd Yevpatoriyan, Red Banner Motor-Rifle Division. By the end of the 1960s, the Division had transitioned into a training unit equipped with a double staff of armoured vehicles, weapons and ammunition. In case of war, it was supposed to create two full-bodied divisions on its base. One was already formed and only after training, could it become combat.

The second was supposed to be staffed by the mobilised local population. For this purpose, it intended to use the second portion of weapons and ammunition stored in the arsenals. In 1987, the Division became 173rd Guards Yevpatoriyan, Red Banner District Training Centre of Junior Specialists of Motor-Rifle Corps (m/u 28320). The Centre included the following major units of Category B: 70th (m/u 16158) and 71st (m/u 11982) Guards Motor-Rifle Regiments based in Grozny and 392nd Tank Regiment (m/u 61652) with 50th Guards Artillery Regiment (m/u 64684) based in Shali. In addition, there were several separate training battalions, whilst all other units were Category C.

In the missile era, Chechnya hosted only one unit armed with ballistic missiles based between Bamut and Assinovskaya – the 3rd Division/Battalion of 178th Guards Rocket Regiment (m/u 23467), 35th Rocket Division (m/u 34196), operating four silo-based R-12 (8K63U, NATO – SS-4 Sandal) Medium Range Ballistic Missiles. Other battalions operating ground based launchers were located in Ingushetia, including 1059th MRTB (Mobile Repair and

Shali based 392nd Training Tank Regiment gate memorial with JS-3 tank pictured in early 1980s. The sign says – Grozny Street (straight), Vedeno (left) and Makhety (right). (Efim Sandler collection)

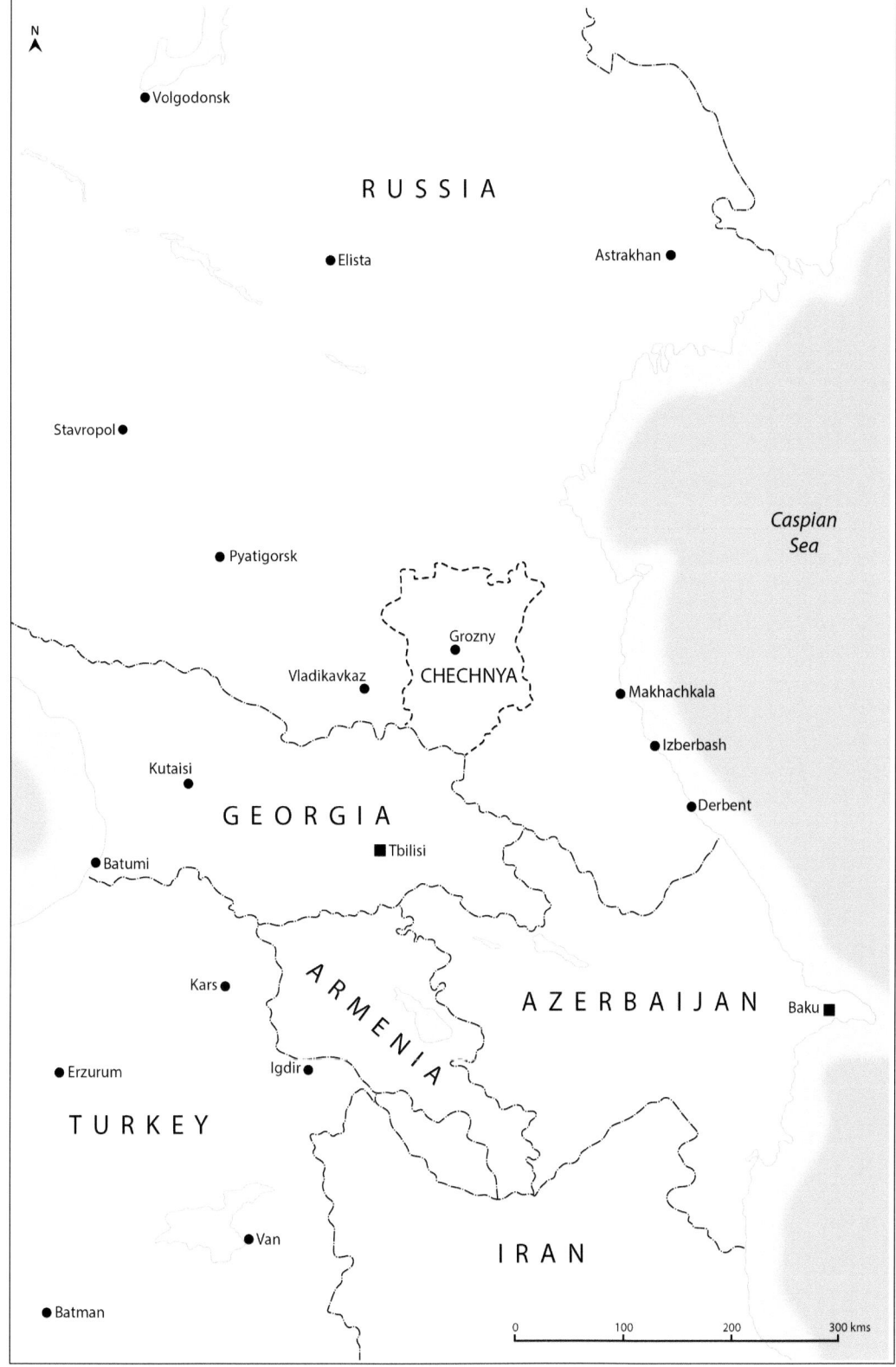

A map of the Chechen Republic, as a part of the Russian Federation and with neighbouring countries of the Caucasus that became independent in the early 1990s. (Map by George Anderson)

Towards Independence

In the late 1980s, Chechnya became involved in the general process of the collapse of the USSR. Ultimately, the Soviet Union had raised its own gravediggers. The most radical parts of society almost universally, turned out to be two segments of the population. On one hand, it was the nationalist intelligentsia, on the other, everyone else. In the USSR, much attention was paid to the creation of cultural and educational institutions on the national outskirts and by doing this, the Soviet administration fell into a trap. Local activists of culture, science and art were by no means always ready to join the Soviet elite – many of them remained loyal to their own national autonomies.

Another social stratum that pushed the republics of the USSR to revolution, was the national bureaucracy. Being the core of the Soviet regime, those people were burdened by dependence on Moscow and preferred to become full-fledged rulers, albeit poor and weak, but of their own estates. The mechanism of events that unfolded in the Chechen-Ingush Autonomous Soviet Socialist Republic did not differ much from what was happening in other national autonomies of the Union.

As elsewhere, isolation did not begin with political slogans. The first rallies in Chechnya were devoted to the problem of building a chemical plant near Gudermes, the second largest city in the republic. In addition to ecology, small informal groups began to discuss ethnologic, historical and other issues, and in 1988, these circles united into a single movement – the Union for the Promotion of Perestroika.

The main advantage of the 'informals' was a radical update of the agenda. Soviet power in its previous form did not suit many people in Chechnya or beyond. The opportunity to discuss once forbidden topics and the expectation of a new life, made it possible to campaign on a grand scale and with colossal effect. There was no intelligible programme, except for the broadly understood democratisation and nationalism of these people. However, in order

Technical Base) – which actually dealt with storage and maintenance of nuclear warheads.

The 3rd Battalion was commissioned in 1963 and deactivated on 20 September 1980, while 178th Regiment was disbanded. Two other regiments of 35th Division were relocated to Barnaul (Altai Region) in 1981 and transitioned to RSD-10 Pioneer.

Exercise with T-55 tank in 70th Guards Motor-Rifle Regiment (m/u 16158) base in Grozny, 1980s. (Photo via 70th Regiment veterans)

Grozny in Soviet outfit of 1970s. The huge wall posters of 'Fathers of Communism' – Lenin, Marx and Engels were common during those times. (Efim Sandler collection)

to capture the attention of the people on streets, at that time, nothing else was required. Interestingly, religion at that time, played only a secondary role.

Beginning in 1989, an urgent expansion of Islam began in the North Caucuses and Checheno-Ingushetia in particular. Over the next two years, 211 Muslim mosques were built and two Islamic universities were opened. As in the nineteenth century, everything that constituted faith faded into the background and Islam came to the fore as a source of aggressive ideology – muridism.

In 1989, an ethnic Chechen, Doku Zavgaev, was elected for the first time as the First Secretary of the Republican Committee of the Communist Party. He also headed the Supreme Soviet of the Republic. The new head of Chechnya was not a staunch nationalist but he had a good sense of the mood of the masses and tried to ride the wave of public opinion. He quickly consolidated power in his hands, but not everyone liked his rule as Zavgaev proved to be just another Soviet bureaucrat, accused of corruption and placement of relatives in key positions in the republic.

At the same time, Zelimkhan Yandarbiyev came to the fore in Chechen politics. A philologist by profession, he wrote mediocre poetry and headed a literary circle in Chechnya. Although later this man attributed to himself some dissident views, he was the child of the Soviet system of nurturing national cadres. Before entering his first roles in Dudayev's Chechnya, Yandarbiev worked in the Writers' Union of the USSR, was a member of the Communist Party and even during a period of deep stagnation, published his collections of poetry.

Doku Zavgaev, an old bureaucrat, wanted to first get within the existing system. Yandarbiev saw a broader perspective. He founded the Vainakh Democratic Party, which aimed to turn Chechnya into a union republic within the USSR. Chechnya, as an autonomy, was part of the RSFSR, and the Yandarbiev Group demanded that its status be upgraded to a full-fledged republic, like Georgia or Ukraine.

In 1990, in order to bypass Zavgaev and seize the initiative, Yandarbiev and his supporters decided to organise the Congress of Chechen People. Unfortunately for the unaccomplished journalist, Yandarbiev, did not fit the image of a Mountain People Leader – he needed more aggressive supporters. At this point, Yandarbiev contacted Dzhokhar Dudaev who had just became the first Chechen general and commanded 326th Heavy Bomber Aviation Division headquartered in the Estonian town of Tartu.

Despite widespread opinion, Dudaev was not really known in Chechnya, besides his promotion to the rank of Major-General being reported in the local newspaper. He had spent most of his life outside of Chechnya, rarely visiting his family. He hardly could speak Chechen and was married to a Russian woman who was the daughter of one of his superiors. None of this mattered to Yandarbiev's team, it was more important that Dudaev was the first Chechen military star plus he had aggressiveness and the ability to speak with great confidence and power. During the Congress, Dudaev had been introduced to a number of key people active in the national arena, as well as to members of the Council of Elders. From this point onwards, his political career started to sky-rocket.

AVIATION IN CHECHNYA OF THE SOVIET TIMES

In 1925–26, the first airplanes appeared over Chechnya during expeditions to the Northern Caucuses tasked with battling locust in the rivers of Dagestan. Since 1930, members of the OSOAVIAKHIM organisation started to work on an improvised aircraft ground in the vicinity of Grozny. This evolved into a commercial airfield in 1932 and later became Grozny Airport (old). On 17 February 1938, the first aviation unit based in Chechnya was established – 221st Aviation Detachment of Special Applications formally reporting to Azov-Black Sea-Caucasian Directorate of Civil Aviation. The detachment, also known as Grozny Aviation Enterprise or Grozny Aviation Detachment, operating R-5 and Po-2s, was tasked with liaison and postal duties, medical assistance and less well-known – NKVD service of border control.

Eventually, the unit remained operational on paper only and did not have any aircraft or proper airfield equipment delivered. In 1939, NKVD Chairman, Lavrentiy Beria, reported to Joseph Stalin about the situation with air assets of NKVD and proposed to decommission all of them and transfer the responsibility to the military. On 29 July 1939, Grozny Aviation Detachment was disbanded.

During the war, the units based in the Northern Caucuses were constantly changing, for example, during the Battle of Caucuses (July 1942 – October 1943), Grozny Divisional Air Defence District was established as part of Transcaucasian Air Defence Zone. During the first stage of Battle of Caucuses, July – December 1942, Grozny hosted elements of the 105th Fighter Aviation Division responsible for the District and later, in the second stage, January – October 1943, elements of 126th Fighter Aviation Division were based there.

Great Patriotic War

During the Great Patriotic War, many Chechens fought bravely and distinguished themselves in combat against the German invasion. One of them was the first Chechen pilot, Major Dasha Akaev. Born on 5 April 1910, in Shalazhi Village of Urus-Martan District, Akaev was accepted into the First United Civil Aviation Pilot School in Biysk and graduated in 1933 as a pilot of agricultural aviation assigned to Transcaucasian Directorate of Civil Aviation. In 1934, he enrolled in the Military Pilot School in Odessa and after graduation, began service in the Naval Aviation unit in Eisk.

When the war started, Akaev was serving in 117th Aviation Regiment of Amur Flotilla, flying MBR-2 and U-2. He was promoted to 3rd Squadron Deputy Commander in January 1942 and reported to 58th Separate Aviation Squadron of Baltic Fleet flying MBR-2, received a rank of a Captain and awarded Order of Red Star. In late 1942, Akaev attended training on Ilyushin Il-2 aircraft and was assigned to 35th Assault Regiment of 9th Assault Aviation Division of Baltic Fleet. In September 1943, he was promoted to rank of Major and became Regiment Commander. During the Leningrad Frontier offensive to lift off the blockade of Leningrad, Akaev distinguished himself as brave and skilled commander and was recommended for the very prestigious Order of Alexander Nevsky but instead, he was awarded the Order of Red Banner.

From the award commendation:

During the operation to break through the fortified defence line of the Germans south of Mt. Oranienbaum, Major Akayev personally made seven successful sorties for the destruction of enemy manpower and equipment.

14 January 1944 – made two sorties, as a result of which in the villages of Kopylovka and Dyatlitsy destroyed one tank, knocked out one armoured vehicle, suppressed the fire of small AAA batteries and destroyed up to 20 soldiers and officers.

17 January 1944 – twice led groups of four to seven IL-2 aircraft, while destroying up to 20 soldiers and officers at Elizavetino Station. In the village of Kipen, he destroyed an artillery battery up to 10 bunkers, eight wagons with manpower and five horses. Confirmed by crews and photo.

18 January 1944 – leading seven IL-2 aircraft with a bombing attack on the village of Vitino, destroyed seven vehicles, four wagons, up to two companies of infantry.

19 and 20 January 1944 – performed sorties of a bombing strike with reconnaissance in Ropsha District, Yuryevo, as a result destroyed eight vehicles, 12 wagons with manpower and up to 80 soldiers and officers.

Following the deportation of Chechens on 23 February 1944, Akaev was subjected to immediate decommission and deportation. However, the commander of the 9th Division, Colonel Georgy (Nodar) Hatiashvili, taking a huge risk, managed to save and keep him in the unit. Following the events, Dasha Akaev, suffered from severe depression but continued to perform his duties in the best way possible. He personally worked out the operation to destroy a heavily defended airfield in Rakvare (Estonia) that was of paramount importance for Germans in the area.

On 26 February 1944, he personally led the strike force of several groups. His Il-2 was shot down and crashed into German positions. Akaev and seven of his men died in the attack but the 35th Regiment accomplished the mission: Rakvare airfield was put out of action and was not operational again until captured and repaired by Soviet troops. For his actions, Daka Akaev was recommended for a Title of Hero of Soviet Union (twice): his name was erased from the list and he never received any award.

The Cold War

After the war, Soviet Army experienced at least four massive reorganisation iterations – in 1946, 1949, 1954 and 1960. Huge numbers of units were relocated, merged, decommissioned and reorganised so it is very hard to track them as the enumeration did not have any kind of order or logic.

On the Caucuses, two major military structures were formed in 1946 – Transcaucasian Military District and North-Caucasian Military District (the latter included the territory of Chechnya previously belonged to Stavropol Military District). Both structures had respective aviation assets in form of 7th Air Army and VIII Fighter Aviation Corps of Air Defence (aka Baku Corps), as well as 11th Air Army headquartered in Tbilisi. Around the same time, a newly organised XLII Fighter Aviation Division of Air Defence Corps took responsibility over the Chechnya-Ingushetia area with its 382nd Fighter Aviation Regiment based in Khankala, near Grozny.

A line of L-29 Dolphin training jets of 382nd Training Aviation Regiment of Stavropol High Military Aviation College of Pilots and Navigators at Khankala airfield, 1971. (photo by Alexander Shkrab)

MiG-15UTI of Grozny Training Aviation Center of DOSAAF pictured in 1981. Note the 'DOSAAF' marking can be clearly seen under the cabin. (via GTAC veterans)

ended and the jets started to arrive to Caucasian units, mainly used for transitional training. From 1949 till 1951, Vladimir Komarov served as a Senior Pilot in one of the Squadrons of 382nd Regiment.[1]

The next round of changes started in 1954. On 3 July 1954, North-Caucasian Air Defence Army was formed and based on IX Corps of Air Defence (aka Stalingrad Air Defence District), headquartered in Rostov-on-Don. Among others, it included 42nd Division (m/u 22215, HQ Grozny) with three fighter regiments – 382nd (m/u 22467, Khankala), 389th (m/u 19017, Gudermes) and 676th (m/u 55038, Sleptsov – Ingushetia), whilst all regiments were transitioning to MiG-17s. It is important to note that previously, 676th Warsaw, Red Banner, Fighter Aviation Regiment based in Pirsaat (Azerbaijan) reported to 216th Fighter Aviation Division and took part in the Korean War from 25 July 1952, till 27 July1953.

In 1960, the Soviet military experienced another revision and all the Air Defence assets were reformed under Baku Air Defence District. The North-Caucasian Army of Air Defence was reformed into XII Corps of Air Defence, headquartered in Rostov-on-Don, 42nd Fighter Aviation Division was reformed into 22nd Division of Air Defence with only one aviation regiment – 382nd. Meanwhile, 676th transferred to Category B and was put on storage and 389th was disbanded and reformed as 1124th Anti-Aircraft Rocket-Artillery Regiment, reporting to 9th Division of Air Defence, with homebase in Kramatorsk (Donetsk Oblast), operating S-75 SAMs.

In 1963, the 10th Division of Air Defence joined the District arriving from Cuba, with 815th Anti-Aircraft Rocket-Artillery Regiment operating five battalions of C-75s with HQ in Grozny. In the mid-1960s, 22nd Division has been relocated to Norilsk and 382nd Regiment, with all its support units, was inherited by Armavir High Military Aviation College of Air Defence in around 1967. Shortly, the regiment started transitioning to L-29 training jets which was completed by 1969.

The next round began in 1949 when the aviation assets in the Caucuses were reorganised into XLII Fighter Aviation Army of Air Defence Corps, XXI Fighter Aviation Army of Air Defence Corps and 34th Air Army of Air Force. The 42nd Army included XXXVI Fighter Aviation Corps that in turn, included 42nd Division headquartered in Grozny with the already mentioned, Khankala based 382nd Regiment and newly formed 389th Fighter Aviation Regiment based in Gudermes, both operating MiG-15 jets.

During the same period, the Soviet military – and Aviation in particular – were busy with the introduction of new weapons. From April to September 1950, 382nd Regiment of 42nd Division, commanded by the Hero of the Soviet Union, Lieutenant-Colonel Alexey Logvinenko, conducted operational trials of Yak-23 fighters, performing 2,176 sorties (34 night sorties), with a total flying time of 990 hours (22 hours of night time). Ironically, Yak-23 was already committed for production before the trials

Soon afterwards, the newly formed Stavropol High Military Aviation College of Pilots and Navigators of Air Defence Corps, took over the assets in Khankala which included 382nd Training Aviation Regiment, 95th Separate Battalion of Airfield Support and 1203rd Separate Battalion of Communications, Radio-navigation and Aircraft Landing.

In 1975, the unit was the first one in the USSR that started to operate newly arrived L-39 training jets. By the Directive of the General HQ No. 314/5/01040 of 14 August 1991, 382nd Training Aviation Regiment with its support units was transferred to Armavir College. De facto Armavir College never had a chance to take over the unit as it was busy absorbing units withdrawing from Azerbaijan. Stavropol College continued to use the jets in very limited mode until all personnel left Chechnya in 1992.

Stavropol College was the first in the USSR to operate L-39 Albatross training jets. The newly arrived aircraft seen in Khankala airfield in 1974. (via Stavropol High Military Aviation College veterans)

Civil Aviation

In 1945, the 221st Detachment was reactivated and in 1946, started operations flying Po-2 biplanes. At the time, there were two Po-2 airplanes but one of them crashed in February 1947, killing the pilot. In 1952, the detachment was reformed as 82nd Aviation Detachment of North-Caucasian Territorial Directorate of Civil Aviation and in 1954, the first An-2s started to arrive –at first employed in An-2T and An-2SKh variations. In 1957, Eli Khakimov became the first Chechen member of the detachment after graduating from Krasno-Kut Flying College of Civil Aviation.

In 1959, the first helicopters Mi-1 and Ka-15 started to arrive in Grozny giving a push to the growth of the detachment. On 27 June 1963, upon the Order of General Directorate of Civil Aviation, Grozny United Aviation Detachment was formed, comprising 82 Detachment and Grozny Airport facilities. The new unit operated Yak-12, An-2, Mi-1 and Ka-15/18 aircrafts. At the same time, more Chechen pilots joined the detachment – Mukharbi Chokuev, Khamid Yandiev and Anderbek Akhmatov. In 1968 An-10 and An-24 started in operation for passenger flights.

The 1970s marked a blossoming of Civil Aviation in Chechnya with the introduction of new passenger carriers – Yak-52 (1972)

Po-2S 'CCCP-K1427' of Grozny Aviation Detachment seen in Nalchik, Kabardino-Balkaria, in 1956. (Alexander Kolesnikov collection, via Efim Sandler)

A fine image of DOSAAF Yak-52 of Grozny Training Aviation Center pictured in 1970s. Note the DOSAAF marking on the tail. (Efim Sandler collection)

and Tu-134 (1977). The detachment, from 1974 headed by Gennady Kruglikov, managed to transfer pilots from An-2 to Tu-134 in a very short time and on 2 February 1978, performed the first commercial flight along the route Grozny-Ashkhabad-Makhachkala. At the same time, the construction of a new airport complex started – Grozny-Severny (North). By 1985, with the new airport active, the Detachment Fleet included seven Tu-134s and 34 An-2s, plus there were over 30 pilots, navigators and onboard technicians of Chechen and Ingush nationalities.

On 20 October 1986, the Grozny Detachment was involved in one of the most bizarre aviation disasters in the history of the Soviet Civil Aviation. On this day, Flight 6502 from Sverdlovsk to Kuibyshev (Samara), operated by Grozny 82nd Detachment Tu-134A, registration CCCP-65766, departed to its destination at 14:33. Just before the departure, the commander had a dispute with the 2nd Pilot and in order to prove his skills, decided to perform an instrumental landing with no visuals, in total defiance of the Civil Aviation Operating Procedures. At 15:31, the commander started the descent with the shade covering the windshield and misjudged the descent speed and distance all the while neglecting calls from the ground control. At 15:50, the airplane touched the runway on the right chassis at 280km/h and a descent rate of 5m/sec, then hit the runway on the left chassis while the left wing suffered 4.8G force and started to disintegrate releasing the fuel. The jet continued to run for about 200m and then flipped over, dragging itself to the side off the runway. The whole body of the plane stopped and a fire erupted, destroying the plane and killing 70 passengers and crew.

In 1992 Grozny Detachment ceased to exist and was succeeded by the national company, STIGL.

Grozny DOSAAF Aviation Training Centre

The first aviation training centres began to emerge in the early 1960s based on the USSR DOSAAF aviation sports clubs. The Centre was divided into aircraft and helicopter centres, and those, in turn, were divided into centres of the first stage of training and centres of the second stage of training. Aircraft centres of the first stage of training trained cadets on L-29 Dolphin jet trainers, aircraft centres of the second stage trained cadets on MiG-15UTI and MiG-17 jet trainers (since 1985 they wanted to replace them with MiG-21 but was replaced by the L-39 Albatross). Helicopter centres of the first stage of training trained cadets on Mi-1 helicopters, helicopter centres of the second stage of training trained cadets on Mi-2 and Mi-4 helicopters.

The first-year cadets attended five months of theoretical studies (from November to March) and six months of practical training that included 50–60 hours of flight time (from April to September). After completion of the first year, they received the rank of a Sergeant of Reserve and attended medical evaluation upon the standards of fighter aviation pilots. During the second year, the cadets received additional theoretical knowledge of combat applications (November-December) and practical training with another 50–60 hours of flight time (January-March). After graduation they received the rank of Junior Lieutenant of Reserve.

Grozny Aviation Training Centre (GATC) was one of the first in USSR, established in 1960 and started operations in about 1963. GATC was the second-year type and operated a mixture of MiG-15 and MiG-17 jest while some L-29 were also spotted in its premises. All the commanders were regular officers of the Air Force and all the instructors were reserve officers attending military duties. The Centre was based in Kalinovskaya airfield that by 1991 hosted several types of fighter jets used for ground training purposes – MiG-21, MiG-23, MiG-19, Su-15, et cetera. For the parachute training several An-2 were used and probably a couple of Mi-8 helicopters. In 1991, GARC has been deactivated along with all other centres in order to give space for the military units withdrawing from Eastern Europe and ex-Soviet republics.

6
ARMING CHECHNYA

One of the major parts in the history of the conflict, is the story of Chechen militarisation. Dzhokhar Dudaev gained popularity and became a Chairman of Executive Committee of the National Congress of Chechen People (OKChN) during its second session in June 1991. He quickly realised that to the perform an effective opposition to the legal authorities of Chechen-Ingush Republic headed by the Supreme Soviet (read – Communists), could only be performed if backed up by force. During that time and with the help of the personal connections of Beslan Gantemirov, ex-Soviet Ministry of Interior NCO and a Chechen entrepreneur, Akhmet Nukhaev, (who specialised in reselling stolen cars with his connections in the criminal world), managed to acquire a certain number of small firearms to start forming 'self-defence' units.

The units were subordinated to Beslan Gantemirov, who was appointed as Chairman of Defence Committee and the units had to be manned by volunteers – preferably those who had service experience in Soviet Army and who often disappeared after several days of training. The first new-born Chechen unit was named Special Forces Company of National Guard of Chechnya and its first commander was Ruslan Shamaev, a retired NCO of Internal Troops Special Forces unit located in Fergana, Uzbekistan (probably element of 3rd Separate Operational Brigade, m/u 3661). He was introduced to Gantemirov when he visited Grozny on holiday, who in turn introduced him to Dudaev and the latter offered him the position of commanding officer.

The first action took place on 23 August 1991, when Gantemirov's men took over the State TV building and forced to broadcast the video of Dudaev's proclamations across Chechnya. After two hours, the building was vacated with minimal damage and no casualties.

The formal head of Chechnya, Doku Zavgaev, ordered the Ministry of Interior to arrest the attackers but many Chechens serving in the militia were supporters of Dudaev and the order was never fulfilled.

On 2 September, Shamil Basaev joined the unit. Basaev had just arrived from Moscow where he took part in defeating the August Coup and was eager to join the events in Grozny. He signed up for the Guard and demanded a platoon commander position – although having no military experience, he brought with him a bag with an AK rifle and hand grenades. This seemed a reasonable argument and he was given the platoon while all other platoon commanders were ex-NCOs with Afghanistan experience.

The next month, the company was busy with training, shrinking from an initial 150 men to barely 70 and by October, there were only 50. At this time, another future Chechen military leader joined the unit – Umalt Dashaev who became an instructor of hand combat due to his experience with karate.

On 5 October, the new unit was tasked with capturing the KGB building. The plan included deception, attacking the MVD building and the real objective. At around 12:30 a crowd of 200 unarmed men rushed into the MVD building on Ordzhanikidzhe Parkway. The only guard was promptly disarmed and the main hallway was completely ruined by breaking whatever could be broken.

Later, about 50 men armed with 34 pieces of firearms, approached the KGB building which was located several dozens of metres from the ill-fated MVD. The doors were open and there were only four people inside the building with one weapon. Without any difficulties, Shamaev, Basaev and Dashaev, took over and started to search for weapons. At first there were 12 AK rifles and several boxes of ammunition and hand grenades but in the basement, there was much more – about 100 AK and four SVD sniper rifles. However, one of the Chechens advised them to keep looking as he believed there were more rooms.

Chechen militants of Ruslan Shamaev posing with their trophies after storming the Republican KGB building on 5 October 1991. (via Republic of Ichkeria History Group)

He climbed the ventilation pipeline and managed to sneak into a secret room that was blocked by a wall – there was treasure! 524 AK rifles, 76 machine guns, nine anti-tank rocket launchers, 20 hand grenade launchers, 50 binoculars, 50 night-vision devices, 5,000 hand grenades and about 600,000 rounds for rifles. In addition, there was a stock of supplies, enough to equip about 600 men. At this point, Dudaev took the weapons to claim his superiority. There are questions of how and why, but it seems obvious that the KGB arsenal has been provided to Dudaev by some '3rd Force' that is still not known by this day.

Assault on Grozny No. 0

On 1 November 1991, after winning mock elections, Dzhokhar Dudaev became the President of Chechen Republic. Boris Yeltsin appointed a Presidents Envoy in Chechnya, Akhmet Arsanov, who previously served as Deputy Minister of Forests of Chechen-Ingush Republic. Arriving in Grozny, Arsanov did not try to conduct any kind of meaningful coordination with Dudaev's team simply as Arsanov was not fit for the job. Instead, he started to broadcast very emotional reports of the total collapse of legal Chechen authorities overrun by Dudaev militants.

On 7 November, under pressure from the Vice President, Alexander Rutskoy, President Boris Yeltsin signed Decree No. 178 declaring a State of Emergency in the Chechen-Ingush Republic.

The runway in Grozny airport blocked by trucks during the failed attempt to take over Dzhokhar Dudaev by the force of Ministry of Interior on 8–11 November 1991. (Author's collection)

Rare shots of the hijacked Tu-154B, Flight 63-17, in Atatürk Airport of Ankara, Turkey. On the very left side is Shamil Basaev (purple jacket). (via Efim Sandler)

at the same time, the Presidents' team was busy working out the means of enforcing law and order including legal methods and the use of force. The newly appointed Deputy of Minister of Interior, General Vyacheslav Komissarov, refused to enforce the Decree, reasoning that not all means had been used to achieve a peaceful solution. This was also the position of many other military and militia commanders.

As predicted, the Decree served as a 'red flag to a bull' and Dudaev used it to prompt another round of anti-Russian riots. Dudaev's men started to attack the buildings of the Ministry of Interior, disarming the men and offering them service on the other side. In Moscow, the orders came to deploy 1,200 men of Dzherzhinsky Division of Internal Troops (OMSDON) but its commander, General Vitaly Bosov, refused the orders without proper planning and no heavy equipment and was released from duties.

The force commanded by the Deputy Division Commander, Colonel Oleg Koluzhny, including Special Forces Training Detachment and elements of 2nd Motor-Rifle Regiment, reinforced by Special Motorised Unit of Militia (SPChM) from Vladikavkaz, waited about 8 hours for deployment. A party of about 300 men was flown to Khankala onboard IL-18 transports early on 8 November but the transports with equipment were routed to Beslan and Mozdok. In total, the operation (or improvisation) was supposed to include about 1,200 personnel under the overall leadership of General Komissarov and Colonel Oleg Ovchinnikov, the Head of Department, Internal Troops Command.

At the same time, Dudaev (who possibly received the information of the incoming force) started his preparations – Khankala airport was surrounded by armed men with trucks and tractors ready to block the runway. On the main square in Grozny, a major gathering had been organised including about 100,000 people. Moreover, at around noon, a group of Chechens including Shamil Basaev, Said-Ali Satuev and Lom-Ali Chachaev, hijacked the Tu-154 airliner, Flight 63–17, with 171 onboard on its way from Mineralnye Vody to Ekaterinburg. They directed it to Ankara with the demand to stop 'Russian incursion' into Chechnya.

The idea for the hijacking had come from Satuev who was a civilian pilot flying Tu-134 airliners. Dudaev supported the plan but also recommended to involve Shamil Basaev and his men, who would not hesitate to be involved. Satuev managed the hijacking carefully and the story ended without casualties.

Meanwhile, the planes with Russian forces landed in Grozny and were instantly blocked by Dudaev militants. Also blocked was everybody who was in the garrisons of the Ministry of Interior and KGB, railway stations and roads.

In Grozny, there were 495 men of the Ministry of Interior including the newly arrived joint detachment of OMSDON who were blocked in the airport by a crowd of about 10,000 including 500 armed men. Chechens put heavy trucks on the runway to exclude the option of reinforcements by air, dismantled a part of the railway tracks and put roadblocks on routes.

In Beslan, the group of Internal Troops included 1,018 men, 19 BTRs, 41 trucks and 23 other vehicles who moved towards Nazran. However, the road from Nazran to Chechnya had been blocked by locals and the detachment had to return. The situation around the MVD building was alarming; it was surrounded by a crowd of several thousands. Chechens demanded to hand out all the weapons or otherwise, they threatened to pour fuel and ignite the building. To reinforce these threats, they brought out fuel trucks. Finally, the crowd of about 700 armed with newly acquired weapons from

Colonel Oleg Ovchinnikov was the senior officer in the airport area, eventually he managed to calm down the situation when he went to meet with Dzhokhar Dudaev.

the KGB arsenal, stormed the MVD building forcing all Russian servicemen to hand out the weapons (the total number is unknown as there was a mix of different units but it appears no more than 200, headed by General Komissarov, went to the MVD office straight from Khankala).

Oleg Ovchinnikov went to meet Dudaev and was told that there was no such thing as a State of Emergency and all troops had to give up the weapons. At the same time, Moscow started negotiations with Dudaev, who finally agreed to release men out of Chechnya. By that time, he already knew that Yeltsin's Decree No. 178 had failed the voting by the Supreme Soviet and had not been accepted – leaving no legal base for the Russian troops in Grozny – so de facto, making them hostages. On 11 November 1991 as a gesture of good will, Dzhokhar Dudaev allowed all Internal Troops and MVD forces out of Grozny while keeping their weapons. At this point the operation (or stand-off) was over – the victor was obvious.

Dealing with the Army

On 23 November, Dudaev issued a Decree No. 9, welcoming the cancellation of the State of Emergency and condemned the aggressive actions of Russian leadership towards Chechen people. By the Decree and other actions, he ordered:

4. To control the activities of troops from the Armed Forces of the USSR, Russia, temporarily stationed on the territory of the Chechen Republic, and to organise interaction, send representatives of the President to all units.

5. Minister of Internal Affairs of the Chechen Republic to organise strict control and protection border security. Ensure a strict regime for the stay of foreign citizens on the territory of the Chechen Republic.

...

7. The Ministry of Internal Affairs of the Chechen Republic, through the customs service, to organise special control of all goods transported through the territory of the Chechen Republic by rail to Russia from December 1, 1991.

8. Transfer the Transport Prosecutor's Office and the Railway Transport Police Department to the jurisdiction of the Ministry of Internal Affairs and the Prosecutor's Office of the Chechen Republic from December 1, 1991.

In effect, he sealed Chechnya from the inside and put the movement of any military equipment under his control. On 26 November, Dzhokhar Dudaev called to his office, Commander of 173 District Training Centre (m/u 28320), General Petr Sokolov, Military Commandant of Grozny, Captain 1st Rank Ibragim Deniev and Head of HQ of Civil Defences, Colonel Vaganov. During the meeting he announced all military assets were the property of the Chechen Republic and anyone who would try to cross the border of Chechnya would be arrested. On the next day, Dudaev gave his first interview to Russian reporters of the *Red Star* newspaper and confirmed his intention that Chechens would be ready to fight a war against Russia.

On 30 November, Pavel Grachev, by then the First Deputy Commander of Commonwealth of Independent States (a post-USSR community of ex-USSR republics) armed forces, arrived in Grozny and accompanied by Head of HQ of North-Caucasian Military District, General Anatoly Chernyshov, went to meet Dudaev for the first time. During their conversation, Grachev asked about taking all heavy weapons out of Chechnya – aggressively, Dudaev cut him short saying, 'All weapons belong to Chechen Republic!'

After the meeting and whilst lodging in the 15th Military Compound in Grozny, Chernyshov offered Grachev the opportunity to solve the matter in a fast and dirty manner, right now – he should bring tanks to Grozny and take over Dudaev. He even ordered Petr Sokolov to make arrangements with 392nd Training Tank Regiment (m/u

Commander of 173rd District Training Center, General Pyotr Sokolov, negotiating with Chechen National Guard members regarding taking over the weapons. Grozny, November 1991. (via Efim Sandler)

61652) based in Shali. Grachev agreed on the spot – both knew Chechens did not have anti-tank means. Nevertheless, eventually, he rejected the offer.

Instead, they discussed the option to use force to take 173rd Centre depots and heavy weapons out of Chechnya. The idea was to set-up three convoys with KamAZ trucks and buses for the families of servicemen, escorted by tank battalions moving in three directions – Kizlyar, Nazran and Mozdok. At the same time, OMON and Internal Troops, moving from respective directions, should be brought towards the convoys to ensure protection from locals and clear the roads. Pavel Grachev agreed and reported the plan to Moscow – which never responded.

Russian BMD-1 passing armed Chechen militants near the border with Ingushetia. November 1992. (Photo by Robert Nickelsberg)

Nonetheless, Russian commanders of the North-Caucasian Military District headed by General Lev Shustko, started the work in early December 1991. The first mission of General Chernyshov was to remove all cyphering equipment which he carried out when secretively flying back and forth during 'negotiations'. On the second week of December, Russians started to dismantle or sabotage the targeting equipment on missiles, artillery, tanks and other types of weapons. All specific equipment like night-vision, radio stations, engineering equipment was taken from depots and transferred out of Chechnya or sabotaged. For some reason, the fact that Russian military commanders were going back and forth on transport planes never attracted any attention from the Chechens.

At the same time, the families of servicemen were leaving Chechnya on the same planes. By January 1992 the work on 'voiding' all weapons systems became so massive that even the fuses of bombs and anti-tank mines were replaced with dummies. Additionally, the Russians developed a very complex plan of mining the arsenals. Engineers, many with combat experience, and knowledge and conducted several layers of mining. This work was not authorised and never reported but an example of the actions meant that every single piece of Chechen heavy weaponry taken by Russians in 1994–1995 had either no working targeting device or none at all.

Finally on 4 January 1992, General HQ issued Directive No. 314/3/0159 to disband 173rd Training Centre. On the same day, Russian units started to decommission the equipment and dismantle it. General Shustko ordered the write-off 18 BM-21 Grad, four 9K52 Luna, three 9P148, seven BM-37, six T-62, 35 BMP-1/2, 14 BTR-70, 16 BRDM and four BTS. Little by little, Russians were wasting the equipment that had no chance of leaving Chechnya peacefully. This activity could only be done secretly so as not to attract attentions of Chechen militants who from November 1991, were constantly monitoring Russian military units.

Attacks

The first recorded attack on the Russian garrison occurred on the night of 4–5 January 1992, when several militants seized Access Control Entrance of Signalling Battalion of 339 Radio-Technical Regiment of Air Defence (m/u 03007) based in Khankala. The attackers demanded to open the weapons room but the Officer of Duty, Major Vladimir Chichkan, refused and tried to hit the alarm button but was shot dead. In the coming days, there were several attacks on servicemen and their families until Commander of 173rd Centre, General Sokolov, ordered to distribute weapons to the officers and reinforce security of the bases. After a short pause, the attacks resumed:

- 1 February – several attackers armed with rifles took over and destroyed the communication point of Caspian Flotilla, seizing 100 pieces of small arms.
- 4 February – attack on 566th Regiment of MVD. Seized over 3,000 pieces of weapons and over 184,000 of ammunition.
- 7 February – attack on 93rf Radio-Technical Regiment in Grozny, seized about 150 pieces of weapons.
- 7 February – 15th Military Compound was attacked but was repelled.
- 7 February – attack on 382nd Training Aviation Regiment, over 400 pieces seized.
- 8 February – attacks on 1st and 15th Military Compounds in Grozny – several armour pieces taken.
- 19 February – the depots of Grozny's garrison hospital was annexed by Chechens.

In several cases, when a furious crowd was rushing inside the garrisons crushing everything on its way, Dzhokhar Dudaev personally had to calm them down. In one case, there was a firefight between armed Chechens and Dudaev guars, leaving 10 people dead. The robbery of the military units continued through March and April. On 31 March, Head of Parliament of Chechen Republic, Khusein Akhmadov signed Decree No. 119 ordering to transfer all CIS military units and their equipment under jurisdiction of Chechen Republic (this is actually a serious question – why was such a milestone decree not been issued by Dudaev himself?).

By the end of March, a large portion of weapons and vehicles had been transferred out of Chechnya under the cover of planned exercises. Dudaev's outburst was ferocious – on 1 April, he threatened to execute any Russian servicemen and members of their families who dared to cross the border without permission.

De facto, by May 1992, 70–80 percent of the weapons were taken. Earlier in April, General Boris Gromov had inspected the units of North-Caucasian Military District and reported that there was no peaceful way of getting the weapons out of Chechnya. On 18 May 1992, Pavel Grachev replaced Evgeny Shaposhnikov but still there were no decisive actions from Russian Military Command. The garrisons remained sealed without any supplies as per Dudaev orders. The officers and NCOs managed to get their families into bases for protection. The guard duties were performed mostly by officers and NCOs. Many soldiers, especially of Caucasian nationalities, left the bases often taking whatever weapons they could carry.

Many letters from the officers to Russian authorities – President, Minister of Defence, Chief Prosecutor, et cetera, remained unanswered or received the responses similar to the one from the Assistant of General Prosecutor, Valery Mishin, which stated that, 'due to anti-constitutional nature of Prosecutor Office in Chechen republic and its illegal appointments, making General Prosecutor Office unable to perform required investigation.'

On 28 May, Pavel Grachev issued a Directive to Commander of North-Caucasian Military District, Lev Shustko, No. 316/1/0308sh where he ordered to transfer 50 percent of heavy weapons to Chechen Republic. In turn, Dudaev agreed to let all servicemen and their families out of Chechnya. This was accomplished on 6 June 1992 bringing with them over 11,000 pieces of weapons. Chechen did not allow the removal of any kind of heavy weaponry; for example, they blocked the runways of the airbase in Khankala. The number of weapons received by the Chechens was astronomical for the small republic (note the numbers vary from source to source thus, the numbers are approximate):

- 42 tanks (T-72A/B, T-62M)
- 110 APC (BMP, BTR, MTLB, BRDM)
- 150 artillery systems (2S3, D-30, MT-12, BM-21, BM-37, mortars)
- 100 ATGMs (Fagot, Metis, Konkurs)
- 500 RPG launchers
- 1,000 heavy machine guns
- 27 AAA pieces (ZU-23-4, ZU-23-2 and S-60)
- 57,000 automatic and small arms

As mentioned earlier, the majority of heavy weapons were lacking essential equipment; for example, the V-750 missiles of two S-75 Dvina complexes (NATO SA-2 Guideline), shown several times during parades in Grozny were no more than useless metal junk. The same was true for 9K52 Luna-M (NATO FROG-7) and even one piece of 9K79 Tochka (NATO SS-21 Scarab) – probably a training mock-up.[1]

7
ARMED FORCES OF ICHKERIA

Apart from the well-known units RDB of Shamil Basaev or Borz of Ruslan Gelaev, the story of Chechen military forces in the early 1990s is barely known as all others have been mainly forgotten. There is barely any documentation and much was destroyed during the continuous war, while the majority of participants are no longer alive. The following reconstruction is primarily based upon recollections of veterans and several journalists underway in Chechnya of the 1990s.

Elite Units
As mentioned earlier, the first Chechen units were established before Dzhokhar Dudaev became president and there existed a paramilitary unit called the Special Forces Company of National Guard of Chechnya, commanded by ex-Soviet NCO of Internal Troops Special Forces, Ruslan Shamaev and reporting to Beslan Gentemirov. The unit included four platoons, commanded by Shamil Basaev, Umalt Dashaev, Moh'yadi Susurkaev and an unidentified member nicknamed 'Major'. The first action of the unit was storming the KGB compartments in Grozny on 5 October 1991. After becoming President, Dzhokhar Dudaev ordered all residential armed elements (read gangs) to disband and by the Decree of 2 November No. 12 signed by Head of Parliament, Khussein Akhmatov, formed a National Guard, appointing Magomed (Ruslan) Shamaev as its commander. The National Guard (NG) were mostly volunteering units but the NG Special Forces was a professional unit. The National Guard reported to the General HQ headed by Aslan Maskhadov, ex-Soviet, armed forces colonel, in his last position as Chief Rocket and Artillery Officer of VII Army Corps.

The Chechen Presidents Guard grew up from personal Dzhokhar Dudaev security guards which numbered only seven by October 1991. The first commander was Movladi Dzhabrailov from Staraya Sunzha, ex-MVD officer and the owner of a black belt in karate, and his deputy became Masud Bamatgiriev. The unit soon grew to 14 who were either in the President's Palace near Dudaev's office or in the Katayama District of Grozny where he lived with his family.

After Dudaev became President, the President's Guard started to recruit more people and soon there were about 200 candidates who started training in a former School of Militia, leaving about 130 men. A group of 30 men reportedly went to Pakistan but this is very unlikely as during that period, the budget was tight and connections with other Islamic communities were still undeveloped.

The Presidents Guard camped in the 2nd Military Compound after the Russian forces left and had a hard time defending the assets from the armed Chechen looters. The President's Guards included two branches – President Security – the bodyguards, and Special Forces, also called 'President's Berets'. The peak number in the President Guard was about 150 men.

Special Forces Regiment Borz was formed from the Chechens who fought in Abkhazia and commanded by Ruslan Gelaev. The unit was based on the same compartment as the unit of Shamil Basaev and at first, was named the Separate Battalion of Special Forces, reporting directly to Dudaev. The date when the unit was officially formed is considered to be 20 February 1993. At this point, Gelaev had men but no homebase, Basaev had the base but most of his unit disappeared and his place was wasted. As a result, Basaev offered Gelaev a resort for the new unit. Gelaev was a fan of Special Units –

Shamil Basaev and Dzhokhar Dudaev visiting the National Guard unit in summer 1992. Note, Basaev was never a fan of fancy uniforms and preferred Soviet style camouflage. (via Republic of Ichkeria History Group)

he watched movies about Afghanistan and Vietnam and read books. He was obsessed with the idea of creating a universal unit. His men were training with tanks and APCs, all kinds of weapons and even basic flying with helicopters. In Abkhazia, he started to practice a mobile war with small groups of 12–24, men armed only with small weapons. Much of his experience was deployed during the defence of Grozny in 1994–95. The insignia of the Regiment was a green beret and a member could earn it after showing fine skills and taking part in real combat.

In late 1993, after Shamil Basaev and his men had returned from Abkhazia, he formed the Reconnaissance-Diversionary Battalion (RDB) that consisted of about 60 men, all of them combat veterans. In December 1993, Basaev, Gelaev and several other commanders, opposed Dzhokhar Dudaev's policy of budget cuts and demanded new elections. By then, Dudaev had excluded them from the armed forces. The compelling event was the newly formed and sponsored by, Russia opposition. On 10 August 1994, Dudaev invited Shamil Basaev and offered him to create the unit while being appointed its commander – the RDB returned to being a part of the Chechen Armed Forces. The core of the battalion were the same 60 men who came with Basaev from Abkhazia but in peak times, the unit was ramped up to 270 men.

Shali Tank Regiment

In general, the Shali-based 392nd Tank Regiment (m/u 61652), commanded by Lieutenant-Colonel Sergey Makarov, was fortunate as the new-born local authorities, led by Saypudi Isaev, were keen not to let Dzhokhar Dudaev hand over their homeland and they saw the Russians as their allies. In short, they were probably the main factor preventing the Chechens having more tanks and other weapons and allowing the Russian military personnel to leave Ichkeria in peace.

Nevertheless, about 30 training tanks were left to the Chechens as a bribe for granting safe passage for the men of the 70th Motor-Rifle Regiment out of Chechnya. In total, the 392nd Regiment left 38 T-72 and four T-62 tanks mostly from the educational units. Out of these, 11 T-72 and one T-62 were junk and the Chechens only managed to acquire 19 operational tanks (16 T-72A and three T-62 mod 1972). Eventually, Makarov and his commanders managed to move some of the tanks, armoured vehicles and other weapons out of Chechnya under the disguise of an exercise.

According to the plan presented by Aslan Maskhadov to Dudaev, the Regiment was to be developed into a Mechanised Brigade with following organisation:

- 3 tank battalions
- 1 motor-rifle battalion
- 1 artillery battalion
- 1 rocket-artillery battalion
- 1 engineering battalion
- 1 maintenance battalion
- 1 anti-tank company
- 1 reconnaissance company
- 1 signals company
- 1 anti-aircraft company
- 1 medical detachment

Not much of the plans came to light – the Shali Tank Regiment remained a battalion size unit. The most problematic issue was the lack of trained crews and only one to two companies were activated. Moreover, there was no well-defined unit structure. Despite all of this, Shali's regiment evolved as a part of the Ichkeria forces in 1993, under the command of local chief – Saypudi Isaev, but due to his disagreement with

The first group of Shamil Basaev's (sitting with the hat) newly formed Reconnaissance Diversionary Battalion (RDB) just after his return from Abkhazia. Standing third from the left is Khamzat Khamkarov – one of the most promising Chechen political and military leaders, killed in Grozny on 13 June1994 while leading the fight against Ruslan Labazanov militants. (via Republic of Ichkeria History Group)

Dzhokhar Dudaev, he left his role in mid-1994 and handed it to Issa Dalkhaev (KIA in Jan 1995). Other elements in the regiment were the Mechanised Infantry Company and Anti-Tank Company.

Besides tanks, Shali's Regiment had one or two 2S1 and one 2S3 SPGs, several BM-21 Grad and two ZSU-23-4 Shilkas. During the fights with the opposition in September – November 1994, the regiment enjoyed some additions like opposition T-62s captured in Argun and T-72As from the ill-fated assault on Grozny of 29 November 1994, bringing the number of tanks to between 40 and 50.

The first Chechen military badges and patches of 1992–93 were self-crafted or produced in very small quantities in private within the workshops of Grozny factories. (Efim Sandler collection)

Dzhokhar Dudaev was not very optimistic regarding the performance of the regiment but it did fairly well on the parades. A 2S3 was lost during a training exercise when the ammunition exploded inside the vehicle, the remaining 2S1 self-propelled howitzers (SPHs) and Shilka self-propelled anti-aircraft guns (SPAAGs) were very limited in ammunition and by the beginning of hostilities, most of it was spent.

Ground Forces Orbat

As far as can be established, by the beginning of hostilities, the Armed Forces of Ichkeria were formed as following:

- General HQ (Aslan Maskhadov)
- HQ Battalion
- National Guard (Iles Arsanukaev)
- Special Forces of National Guard (Ruslan Shamaev)
- Presidents Guard (Adam Dudaev)
  ◊ Security Service (Abu Arsanukaev)
  ◊ Special Forces of Presidents Guard (?)
- Special Forces Regiment 'Borz' (Ruslan Gelaev)
  ◊ Separate Special Forces Battalion 'Borz' (Umalt Dashaev)
- Separate Battalion of Special Operations (Akhmed Zakaev)
- Reconnaissance-Diversionary Battalion (Shamil Basaev)
- Shali Tank Regiment (Issa Dalkhaev)
  ◊ Anti-Tank Battalion (Ruslanbek Iderzaev)
- Department of State Security (Sultan Geliskhanov)
  ◊ Battalion of Baisangur Benoevsky (Magomed Khanbiev)
  ◊ Shatoi Battalion (Savladi Beloev)
  ◊ Border Guard Brigade (Vakha Turpulkhanov)
  ◊ Border Guards Special Forces (Viskhan Umakaev)
- Diversionary-Reconnaissance Mountain Regiment (Ayidamir Abalaev)
- Naursk Battalion (Apti Batalov)
- Shali Battalion (Aslanbek Abdulkhadzhiev)
- Shali Battalion (Aslanbek Arsaev)
- Worriers of Islam Battalion (Ali Sultanov)
- Gudermes Battalion (Eli Khamzatov)
- Roshni-Chu Territorial Defence (Akhmad Basunkaev)
- Territorial Defence Detachment (Vakha Arsanov)
- Territorial Defence Detachment (Khunkar Israpilov)
- Islamic Battalion Jamaat (Sheikh Ali Fatkhi)
- Afghan Battalion (Shadid Akhmadov)[1]

Dzhokhar Dudaev visiting Shali Tank Regiment in summer 1993. To his left is Ruslanbek Iderzaev, so-called Mit'ka – commander of the anti-tank unit. (Efim Sandler collection)

Borz Regiment commanders – Ruslan Gelaev (right) and Umalt Dashaev (left) during one of the Special Forces Regiment events, circa summer 1994. Umalt Dashaev was killed during the fighting in Khankala, 28 December 1994. (via Republic of Ichkeria History Group)

- Arab volunteers (?)
- UNA-UNSO Ukrainian volunteers (Sashko Bilyi)
- Melkhistinsk Battalion of Khamzat Khankarov (?)
- Galanchzhoy Regiment (Salam Umalatov)
- Special Forces Regiment of President (Ramsan Umaev)

CHECHEN AVIATION

In December 1993, the Russian leadership decided to pull out all military units from Chechnya while leaving 50 percent of the equipment behind. The locally based aviation assets included

- 382nd Training Aviation Regiment of Stavropol Higher Military Aviation College of Pilots and Navigators, based in Khankala.[2]
- Grozny Training Aviation Centre of DOSAAF (Volunteer Society for Cooperation with the Army, Aviation, and Navy), based in Kalinovsksaya.
- Civilian Grozny affiliate of Aeroflot (82nd Flying Detachment) based in Grozny-Severny airport.

Despite attempts to get most of the serviceable aircraft out from Chechnya, all of them remained where they were. In total, according to the majority of sources, this included about 260 training jets (111 L-39S and 149 L-29), three MiG-17F, two MiG-15UTI and two Mi-8T, plus civilian six Tu-134A, one to two Mi-8, 10 An-2, and a Tu-154B, originally owned by Vnukovo (Moscow), but left in Grozny awaiting repairs after a rough landing. The bulk of military aircraft were sabotaged by the Russians before their withdrawal and had critical assemblies ripped off. According to the Chechens, some of the engines could start but the jets would not take off; no more than three or four were capable of flying and even they lacked some of the gauges and identification friend or foe (IFF) systems.

Ali Matsaev, the most experienced Chechen pilot-instructor, pictured during his service in Soviet Air Force. (Efim Sandler collection)

A well known image of L-39 Albatross in the colours of Ichkeria. The jet was damaged during one of the Russian strikes – probably at Kalinovskaya. (via Efim Sandler)

The situation with spare parts and weapons was also dire. Due to the lack of supplies related to the dissolution of USSR in 1991, the majority of spare sets were wasted, leaving no more 10–15 sets. The majority of aviation munition in 382nd Regiment depots were 'practice', aka concrete filled bomb-shells, equivalent to the weight of the real piece. There were very few UB-16-57 pods for unguided rockets and a small amount of OFAB-50 and OFAB-100 general purpose bombs. Even months later, the Chechens never managed to make more than 10–12 jets capable of flying and the number of flights performed in total was limited to between two and five – also due to the shortage of fuel.

Nevertheless, at least on the paper, the Chechen Air Force included:

A line of L-29 jets in Kalinovskaya in early October 1994. (Efim Sandler collection)

- 1 Attack Aviation Squadron,
- 2 Training Aviation Squadrons,
- 1 Helicopter Aviation Squadron,
- Transport Detachment.

On 24 March 1994, Dzhokhar Dudaev issued an order to prepare crews and four jets – two L-29s and two L-39s – for combat operations. This confirms that those were the only aircraft operational. However, the highest number of L-29s and L-39s see airborne at once, was eight – during the Republic of Ichkeria Independence Day parade on 6 September 1994.

Another and probably more important issue, concerned the availability of quality pilots and mechanical crews. By 1993, Dudaev managed to only attract four people with any kind of flying background, probably by using his personal connections. The most potent was Ali Matsaev, a retired Colonel of Soviet Air Force (1991), who graduated from Yeisk Higher Military Aviation College in 1969 and served on various positions in 116th Guards Fighter-Bomber Air Regiment in East Germany, flying MiG-17F and later Su-7B/BM. In 1981, Matsaev became a student of the Military Academy of General HQ and later graduated from Military-Diplomatic Academy, serving on several HQ positions including Afghanistan and Angola. Despite continuing to fly from time to time, he was not involved in real aerial combat.

Another pilot was reportedly, Khairudi Vesengeriev, who was an ex-DOSAAF instructor flying L-29 and L-39 and was acting commander of the Attack Air Squadron, who received the rank of Lieutenant-Colonel of Russian Air Force. The technical side was managed by Mukhadi Gatsaev, former aviation engineer at Kazan Aviation Plant, working on Tu-22M bombers.

In his interview to the Interfax agency in April 1994, Vesengiriev stated that there were 13 pilot-officers and 30 new cadets who started the theoretical training. Therefore, besides the initial four, the Chechens managed to train (or most probably hire) nine or 10 more pilots. This fact of the presence of several pilots from outside Chechnya, is supported by at least one source, stating that some of them were Russian Airforce officers. There were rumours that several pilots were sent to Turkey for advanced training but this seems very unrealistic.

Nevertheless, the lack of weapons and qualified pilots triggered the idea of using the planes as flying bombs. This was presented in a paper from September 1994 as the 'Lasso Plan' and signed by Dzokhar Dudaev. The plan considered an aerial attack on major infrastructure objectives of nearby Russian cities by all available means. Envisaged as a pure PR action, there were not many details and the document was instantly 'leaked' to the Russian press and initiated 'Chechen Air Force phobia'. This was eagerly supported by Dudaev in a couple of his interviews as he exaggerated his air power to an almost cosmic scale. One should keep in mind that Dzhokhar Dudaev was an experienced pilot and thus the public assumed that he would not overestimate capabilities of his air component.

Meanwhile from the summer of 1994, the Chechen Air Force began to fly sorties against opposition forces. These were mostly performed by a sole L-39 or occasionally, by a pair, using OFAB-50, OFAB-100 and fuel tanks dropped as napalm. Most attacks did not hit their targets, as in all cases, the jets were engaged by AAA and pilots rushed to drop their payload and leave. On 21 September, a Chechen An-2 was hit by AAA and crashed, killing the crew. Reportedly it was performing a routine transport flight for agriculture purposes.

On 3 October, an L-39S was shot down by MANPAD near Goragorsk Village, Urus-Martan District (another version states it was sabotaged and destroyed by an IED placed in the cockpit).

The only known footage of Chechen aviation in action – L-39 Albatross engaging opposition, dropping improvised napalm tanks in summer or early autumn of 1994. The munitions made a huge fireball but totally missed the target. (Efim Sandler collection)

Kalinovskaya airfield of Grozny Training Aviation Center DOSAAF taken from an overflying jet in late 1980s (Efim Sandler collection)

The jet was piloted by an instructor, Ali Matsaev and a cadet-pilot, Dedal Dadaev. Both pilots died. Chechens stated that L-39 was unarmed and was on a weather reconnaissance sortie. In total, it is believed that Chechen jets performed about 20–30 attack missions against opposition forces until 1 December 1994.

In turn, the opposition was supplied by a couple of Mi-8s and a couple of Mi-24s, piloted by Russian crews. The helicopters had no markings and rarely showed themselves, probably due to poor technical condition. On 27 September 1994, an opposition Mi-24V with a Russian crew was hit by small arms near Terskaya village of Northern Ossetia, close to the Chechen border. Attempting to perform an emergency landing on the road, the helicopter flipped over and was destroyed by fire, killing one of the crew. Meanwhile, unidentified jets (obviously Russian) attacked Chechen airbases on several occasions, for example: on 3 October, Kalinovskaya and on 25 November, Grozny-Severny, destroying several planes and damaging the taxiway in Grozny with BETAB bombs. During a November assault on Grozny, Chechen aviation barely showed itself but the opposition's armoured convoys were supported by several Mi-24 gunships with no markings and with uncertain results.

The lack of information gave rise to several myths including fantasy dogfights between L-39s and Su-24s, downing Mi-24 gunships, et cetera. Indeed, nothing close to that ever happened. Both sides lacked any kind of early warning, air control and air-to-air capability.

- Brigade of Internal Troops of Ministry of Interior (Zayndi Mavlatov)
- OMON of Ministry of Interior (Said-Rakhman Bashkaev)

The units of Chechen forces rarely amounted to more than 200–250 men, with the exception of National Guard that could include up to 2,000 men, having detachments all over Chechnya. The majority of so-called 'battalions' did not even reach company size. In total, there were about 15,000 men, not including numerous small local groups that were present in almost every settlement, sometimes consisting of 5–10 men led by a local individual. The exact numbers are not known as well as it is next to impossible to trace small units and their commanders, often known only by their nicknames like 'Major', 'Musa', et cetera. For example, commander of the anti-tank battalion of Shali Tank Regiment, de facto independent unit of a platoon size, Ruslanbek Iderzaev, was mostly known under the nickname (Mit'ka).

Some words should be said about Chechen armed forces uniform and insignia. As of 1994, there was no unified uniform or any kind of insignia in the armed forces. All units either wore civilian clothes or ex-Soviet army apparel from the stocks of 173rd Centre. It can be seen on every image from that period, that all commanders – beginning with Dzkhar Dudaev – wore Soviet uniforms of different types. Very few units, like Gelaev Spetsnaz Borz had personalised items – green berets, or specially designed patches. The badges of the early period varied and showed hardly any logic; they were ordered privately in Grozny based Varzap plant (former Red Sledgehammer – Rus. Krazny Molot), or more commonly, via private sponsors in the Baltic states. The only exception were several sets of parade uniforms for the President's Guard, based on the design chosen by Dudaev and received from Lithuania or Poland in 1994.

8
NOVEMBER RAIN – THE FIRST ARMOURED ASSAULT ON GROZNY

The idea of taking Grozny by force had been discussed in Moscow since the summer of 1993 but nothing happened besides several discussions held at a semi-official level. By the summer of 1994 the situation changed drastically and received top priority attention by President Boris Yeltsin who appointed the Deputy of Nationalities Affairs Minister, Alexander Kotenkov (ex Armour Corps officer), as curator of Chechen opposition. From the summer onwards, Chechen opposition militants began to be trained on the Prudboy range of 33rd Motor-Rifle Regiment, 20th Motor-Rifle Division, near Volgograd.

In August–September, opposition forces, led by Umar Avturkhanov, started to receive heavy weapons – 10 T-62 tanks, 26 BTR-60, four R-145BM, 46 GAZ-66 trucks and several KamAZ trucks loaded with small weapons and ammunition, delivered to Avturkhanov headquarters in Znamenskoe Village. Around the same time, 'unidentified' Su-25 and Mi-24s started to hammer Dudaev forces positions in Argun.

On 13 October 1994, opposition headquarters moved from Znamenskoe Village of Nadterechny District to Tolstoy-Yurt (some 70km to south-east and 15km from Grozny) and started arrangements to move into the city. Moscow was pushing towards the forced solution while, Boris Yeltsin's envoy, Ruslan Khasbulatov and his team, were trying to make it as peaceful as possible – persuading Chechen commanders to stay aside.

It was quite obvious that the Kremlin was using Khasbulatov as decoy to cover its preparations to overthrow Dudaev by force, while opposition leader, Umar Avturkhanov, showed no signs of supporting a peaceful resolution to the crisis. On the same day, Khasbulatov met with several Chechen commanders and proposed a round table meeting of about 10–15 top people to figure out a peaceful solution.

On the morning 15 October, the opposition forces in two parties, led by Umar Avtukhanov and Beslan Gantemirov, attempted the assault Grozny. The main convoy was based on Ruslan Labazanov's forces and included one T-62 tank and a dozen of BTRs followed by GAZ-66 trucks and a long line of private vehicles packed by opposition members. It is important to note that the sole T-62 tank was the only one left from the initial package of 10 tanks – all others were either lost in the skirmishes or had defected to Dudaev.

At about 15:00, two 'unidentified' Mi-24 gunships attacked targets in Grozny and the convoy entered the city moving via Tukhachevsky Street, through the food market and towards the President's Palace. On the other side of the Sunzha River, the detachments of Beslan Gantemirov took over the 15th Military Compartment on the south side and stopped – waiting. At the crossing of Tukhachevsky St. and Sultan Dudaev Boulevard, the convoy was engaged by the men of Shamil Basaev's RDB who managed to set the T-62 and several BTRs on fire by RPGs. Avturkhanov panicked and the whole convoy stopped while firing in all directions. The only person who could manage the situation was Ruslan Labazanov, who ordered his men to take positions in the building of the Fire Department of Ministry of Interior (Tukhachevsky St.). Many opposition members left the city on their own as they decided their leadership clearly had no idea what to do. By the night, the fighting had died down and at about 03:00, the opposition leaders ordered their forces to leave the city.[1]

The assault of 15 October looked like an amateur improvisation without any kind of military consideration. Reportedly, there were hundreds of well-armed opposition men engaged by several dozens of well-trained Shamil Basaev militants spontaneously grouped in the centre of Grozny. It is not clear why Gantemirov's detachment did not join Labazanov's force and nor is it clear why Avturkhanov's convoy became stuck on one street and did not try to bypass from other directions. It is also unknown why opposition leaders ordered to withdraw without any obvious sign of defeat. Accounts mention that the order came from Moscow but the reasons can only be speculated on. However, the assault ended with four (or seven) opposition men killed, five wounded and 14 taken prisoners. One tank and five BTRs were destroyed. The losses to Dudaev's forces are unknown but it is known that Shamil Basaev was wounded in the shoulder.

On 31 December 1993 Dzhokhar Dudaev made his speech with the words: 'Today we are a free nation!' It is believed that this speech marked a point of no-return in Chechen-Russian relations and a countdown to war started. (Author's Collection)

Opposition T-62 tank pictured in Znamenskoe on 5 September 1994. Initially 10 T-62 tanks were supplied but all were either lost or had defected by October 1994. (Photo by Vladimir Sorokin)

tanks with Russian servicemen and intensify the training of Chechen militants in the Prudboy range.

On 1 November, Russian General HQ issued a secret Directive No. 312/1/0130sh, ordering the North-Caucasian Military District to provide Chechen opposition with 40 (or 50) T-72 tanks. Some of the tanks were provided by the 131st Separate Motor-Rifle Brigade from Maikop, some came from 33rd Motor-Rifle Regiment based in Volgograd. The actual number of tanks is not known but in fact, there were no more than 36.

From 3 November, members of the Military Counter-Intelligence Department of FSB, commanded by General Alexey Molyakov, started the hiring process for tank crews from Moscow Military District, under the direct order of the Minister of Defence, Pavel Grachev and with agreement of Moscow Military District CO, Leonty Kuznetsov. The FSB Group responsible for hiring the volunteers, was led by General Karpov, directly working with counter-intelligence officers with respective units. In total, 82 servicemen were hired holding ranks from lieutenant to major and also several NCOs from 4th Guards Kantemirov Tank Division (53 men), 2nd Guards Taman Motor-Rifle Division (3 men), 18th Separate Motor-Rifle Brigade (13 men) and Vystrel Higher Officers Classes (13 men).

Ruslan Khasbulatov instantly switched from a peaceful approach to a de facto forced solution and blamed opposition leaders of being cowards and traitors. Labazanov, in his turn, accused Russian leadership in supplying old weapons, namely T-62 tanks and BTR-60PBs and not providing adequate training (read not sending considerable amount of instructors) to do the job.

Game of Poker

Shortly after the failed attempt of 15 October, the Head of Federal Security Service (FSB) of Moscow and Moscow Oblast, Evgeny Savostyanov, appointed by Yeltsin to oversee Chechnya, conducted a meeting in Mozdok to debrief Chechen opposition leaders on the reasons of failure. During the meeting, Avturkhanov and Gantemirov, supported by Khasbulatov, asked for more heavy weapons, namely tanks and professional crews. The issue of crew preparation was solved very conveniently – it was decided to man

De-jure, the contract between the servicemen and FSB considered only the ferrying of the tanks from Mozdok to Znamenskoe Village for four million Rubles (about $1,300 USD) – one million prepaid and three million after accomplishing the project. In addition, there was an option of taking part in combat actions for five million ($1,620), with a light wound priced at 25 million Rubles ($8,103), a medium wound at 50 million ($16,207), heavy at 75 million ($24,311) and in case of death, the family would receive 150 million Rubles ($48,622).

All hired servicemen were flown from Chkalovskoe airbase to Mozdok, under supervision of Alexander Kotenkon. Besides the tankmen, FSB hired at least three crews for Mi-24 gunships and 40 men of the ex-Special Forces members were tasked with direct combat mission.

The only existing footage of the opposition assault on Grozny of 15 October 1994. The left frame shows a Mi-24 gunship overflying the convoy of opposition forces, next is the member of Dudaev forces operating RPG and on the right, is the smoking T-62 tank that was disabled and later destroyed. (Efim Sandler collection)

The FSB headhunters were not welcome everywhere. Commander of 4th Kantemirov Division, General Boris Polyakov, learned about the issue after his men had already been hired and he tried to interfere by banning them from taking part in this adventuristic activity. His envoy, Colonel Orlov came head-to-head with Alexander Kotenkov at Chkalovskoe airbase but managed to take his servicemen back to the Division. Fatefully on 15 November, Polyakov received a call from the Head of General HQ, Mikhail Kolesnikov, who in a very rude manner, ordered him to send his men to Mozdok.

On 10 November, the decision of moving troops into Grozny was finally approved in Moscow. The FSB team from Chechnya, led by Yunus Tagirov, arrived in Moscow to work out the details of the future operation which, besides opposition forces, was backed up by the massive relocation of Internal Troops towards Mozdok. On the next day, the new (pro-Moscow) Chechen government was formed, led by Salambek Hadzhiev, replacing Akhmed Zavgaev who resigned the same day under the pressure from Umar Avturkhanov.

Grozny, morning 27 November 1994 – it's all over! The operation orchestrated by Russian military commanders failed with catastrophic results. (Photo by Ivan Shlamov)

By 16 November, all newly hired troops arrived at Mozdok and gathered at the 68th Arsenal Base of the Main Rocket and Artillery Directorate (military unit No. 30184) near Mozdok, where the first T-72A tanks arrived. Ironically, none of the Russian tankmen were familiar with T-72 as all of them had been trained on T-80s, however, they started training Chechens to operate the tanks straight away. The Chechens had no prior experience with armour and barely had time to practice – it was decided to have 16 full Russian crews and all others would be mixed.

On 17 November, the first batch of 12 tanks and two trucks, loaded with weapons and ammunition, were ferried from Mozdok to Znamenskoe. On the same day, a large group of Russian officers, led by the Head of General HQ, Mikhail Kolesnikov, arrived in Mozdok. General Gennady Zhukov, Deputy Commander VIII Army Corps, was appointed responsible for the operation from the Russian side but de facto, all decisions were taken by Kolesnikov.

On 18 November, 'opposition' aviation and artillery hammered the positions of Dudaev's forces at Bratskoe Village to ensure a safe pass from Mozdok towards Znamenskoe. The same day, Bratskoe was secured by men of three opposition battalions of Yahya Gerikhanov, Rizvan Tulaev and Usman Satuev.

The final meeting of the operation plan was conducted on 22 November, in Mozdok, under the chairman of Mikhail Kolesnikov and representatives of all involved parties, including the Russian government represented by Alexander Kotenkov, Chechen leaders headed by Umar Avturkhanov and Russian military command – Gennady Zhukov. The plan looked pretty simple – 18 assault groups with armour and infantry would enter Grozny from four directions, two from Priterechye (north and north-east – Avturkhanov forces), Urus-Martan (south-west – Gantemirov forces) and Argun (south-east – Labazanov force), de facto, Labazanov's force hardly included a couple of dozen and potentially, could not control the tanks. Another 18 groups would stay in reserve and join at a later stage.

The operation was planned to start at 04:30 and by 06:00, the troops were supposed to encircle the President's Palace. A separate task was given to two teams of Russian Special Forces – they were supposed to attack Dudaev's Palace using RPO-A Shmels, starting internal fires prior to the arrival of tanks. In total there would be 3,500 – 4,000men of opposition forces including eight battalions (250–500 men each) and several voluntary units from Grozny locals numbered up to 5,000 men. In total, there were 36 T-72A tanks with 24 Russian and 12 Chechen crews, 35 would have to move into Grozny and one should be kept in reserve. The idea of mixed crews has been dismissed despite extensive advice from Chechen

BATTLE FOR GROZNY VOLUME 1: PRELUDE AND THE WAY TO THE CITY, FIRST CHECHEN WAR 1994

Chechen T-72A of Shali Regiment. Shali Tank Regiment was formed under command of Saypudi Isaev, in the second half of 1992, based on the Russian 392nd Training Tank Regiment of 173rd District Training Centre. From the 42 tanks transferred to Chechens, only 19 were in serviceable condition. After the conflict with Dzhokhar Dudaev, who blamed Saypudi Isaev for passiveness during the opposition assault on Grozny in November 1994, Issa Dalkhaev took the command. The tanks remained in the original camouflage with the numbers overpainted. During specific occasions like Dzhokhar Dudaev visits in 1992–94, some tanks were spotted having the Ichkeria national flag painted on the turret. (Artwork by David Bocquelet)

This was the sole T-72B1 in the possession of the Armed Forces of Ichkeria. The tank most likely was taken from 392nd Regiment, although there is no information on the precise case, as reportedly, all tanks of 392nd Regiment were either T-72As or T-62s. This T-72B was seen during the independence parade in Grozny in November 1994 and later, during the fighting around the City. The only notable feature was the Ichkeria national insignia painted on the cover of the searchlight. During the Battle of Grozny, the tank was destroyed by Russian forces. Unlike all other Chechen tanks, it was not painted in white and remained in its original single tone camouflage. Note, the lack of commander machine gun was quite common for Chechen tanks. (Artwork by David Bocquelet)

Towards the Russian operation in December 1994, all Chechen tanks were marked by light colours – white, grey and blue, depending on the availability of the paint. Some had full turret and upper hull painted, others only the sides of the turret. The numbers were also covered by paint. The flags on the Chechen tanks had dual purpose – they were used as national insignia to show a spirit of independence and in order to prevent friendly fire. Note, the latter idea did not work well and all Chechen tanks were destroyed or captured by Russian forces. (Artwork by David Bocquelet)

As a rule, Chechen tanks did not wear any turret numbers but there were several exclusions including the T-72A shown here with the number '600' that was spotted during the fighting in Grozny. The story behind this number is unknown but probably, the tank belonged to either a Regiment Commander or one of the Battalion Commanders. Ironically the '600' can also be attributed to Mercedes-Benz S600 of 1993 – the most prestigious car in Russian Federation and very popular among various criminal establishments and Caucasian gangs, in particular. (Artwork by David Bocquelet)

Starting from November 1994, Russian aviation began attacking targets in Chechnya. Almost every settlement under Dudaev control had its own local defence units that also included anti-aircraft components with improvised gun-truck,s like the pictured UAZ-469, but also used dedicated equipment like ZU-23-2 or S-60 stations. The versatility of such solutions was proven during the fighting with pro-Russian opposition forces and when Russian troops moved into Chechnya. In some cases, the weapons, like S-60, were left unattended in their caponiers as local defenders preferred to flee and were then destroyed by Russians. (Artwork by David Bocquelet)

Another gun-truck of the early period of confrontation was GAZ-66 truck with 12.7mm NSV Utyos heavy machine gun, spotted on several occasions beginning in the summer of 1993. As usually the case for local conflicts, Chechens used whatever they could and in all kinds of ways – for example, such trucks were transporting civilians during the day and were strafing Russian positions during the night. These tactics of disturbance worked well through the whole war. The truck had the Ichkeria national flag painted on the cabin door but did not have overall white as many other vehicles used by Dudaev forces during Russian invasion. (Artwork by David Bocquelet)

One of the Chechen's 'do-it-yourself' was a militarised civilian variation of BRDM-2, ATM-1 Ingul, previously used by either the Ministry of Emergency Situations or the Ministry of Interior. The vehicle was reworked with steel plates covering the rear windows and fit with DShK or KPVT heavy machine gun. The single tone camouflage was applied over the original paint scheme that could still be seen – overall yellow with red strip. One such vehicle was spotted in Grozny in late 1994 and early 1995 during the fighting in Grozny. It is not known how many vehicles existed and what happened to them, but none were ever seen again. (Artwork by David Bocquelet)

In 1992, Dudaev forces received up to 44 of MT-LB armoured vehicles which previously belonged to 173rd District Training Centre. It is not known how many of the MT-LBs were operational by late 1994 but some of those vehicles were fitted with ZU-23-2 stations and used as Infantry Fighting Vehicles (IFV). By the time of the Russian operation in Chechnya, MT-LBs were painted in white and used to defend Grozny, as seen in many news reports – whilst some received overall paint, others had just white turrets. At least two Chechen MT-LBs were either destroyed or captured by Russian forces in early 1995. (Artwork by David Bocquelet)

One the rarest vehicles to see service with the Chechen forces was 2S3 Akatsiya Serf-Propelled howitzer calibre 152mm. There is almost no information about Chechen self-propelled artillery but it is known that Shali Tank Regiment operated 2–3 systems, probably inherited from Russian 50th Guards Artillery Regiment of 173rd District Training Centre. The combination included 2S3 and 2S1 and there is only a single footage of Chechen Akatsiya, taken in Grozny in summer 1993. The vehicle kept the single tone camouflage with no other markings besides a large Ichkeria roundel in black and white. Reportedly, one 2S3 or 2S1 was destroyed during live firing exercise when ammunition exploded. Another vehicle was captured by Russians in the Argun area in early 1995. (Artwork by David Bocquelet)

In 1992, Dzhokhar Dudaev received stocks of obsolete equipment from the Russian units leaving Chechnya. These included several V-750 missiles of S-75 Dvina (NATO SA-2 Guideline) complex, probably from the assets of 815th Anti-Aircraft Missile Regiment that was based around Grozny reporting to 12th Air Defence Corps. The regiment was disbanded in late 1991 during the reorganisation of Air Defence Corps. The missiles were obviously useless, but Chechens fitted them to KaMAZ-4310 series and used them for parades. In September 1993, two civilian KamAZ trucks with V-750 missiles appeared for the first time during a show near Grozny. Later, the missiles were seen on a couple of occasions but towed by trucks in military camouflage. (Artwork by David Bocquelet)

T-62 tank of Chechen opposition forces commanded by Umar Avturkhanov, used during the failed assault on Grozny on 15 October 1994. The troops of Avturkhanov, sponsored by Russia, proved to be incapable of standing against the well trained and experienced Dzhokhar Dudaev units, many of whom were veterans of the war in Abkhazia. On the other hand, one of the opposition commanders, Ruslan Labazanov, blamed Russia for supplying outdated equipment like BTR-60s and T-62s. The tanks had no markings, which was a common situation with Chechen vehicles of the pre-war period, and there was no way to tell which group they belonged to. In some areas, the settlements were controlled by different groups of militants without visible differences, that were in a state of 'cold' peace with each other until a spark happened. (Artwork by David Bocquelet)

Both sides deployed APCs of various types, frequently up-armed with ZU-23-2 automatic cannons calibre 23mm. In this case, the BTR-60 operated by opposition forces of Umar Avturkhanov. The vehicle could be either original BTR-60PB (26 of which supplied) or command version – R-145BM (four supplied) converted to a regular APC. Russia began to supply weapons to opposition forces in summer 1994, including obsolete heavy equipment. The BTR-60s were cursed with many issues including engine problems, communication equipment, et cetera. Various sources suggest that such BTRs were more frequently used in stationary positions rather than IFVs. During the assault on Grozny of October 1994, some of the BTRs had to be abandoned due to technical problems. As usual, opposition armour had no markings at all and kept the regular single tone camouflage. (Artwork by David Bocquelet)

The situation with opposition armour changed towards the ill-fated assault of November 1994. Prior to the operation that was planned and organised by Russian commanders, opposition forces received 40 BTR-80s. All BTRs were drawn from the stocks of the Russian Army and had their regular armament. It is not known how many of these APCs took part in the assault and how many were destroyed or captured. Some of the remaining BTRs were later found by Russian forces in the areas controlled by the opposition. The paint scheme and colours remained in secret up until several hours before the assault then white paint was applied to predefined spots. (Artwork by David Bocquelet)

The 'stars' of the failed November 1994 assault of Grozny, were T-72A tanks operated by Russian crews. They were drawn from several units of the North Caucasian Military District shortly before the assault and were in perfect condition. In total, 36 tanks were supplied and all but one, took part in the operation. From all the tanks that entered Grozny in the late morning of 26 November, only four managed to leave the following night. Others were either destroyed or joined the order of Shali Tank Regiment, maintained by Russian servicemen taking prisoners. The paint scheme used during the assault consisted of white paint applied to tool boxes around the turret. All other markings were erased. (Artwork by David Bocquelet)

T-72A '520' of 9th Separate Tank Battalion (m/u 03842) of 131st Separate Motor Rifle Brigade was a personal mount of the 2nd Tank Company Commander, Captain Victor Ryabovich. Prior to entering Grozny, Captain Ryabovich switched tanks with 1st Platoon Leader tank – T-72A '521'. The tank is in the basic single tone camouflage with 131st Brigade tactical sight and a Russian Federation flag painted on the turret. The numbers of 9th Separate Tank Battalion were 51x, 52x and 53x of 1st, 2nd and 3rd Companies respectively, whilst '500' was the personal mount of 9th Battalion CO, Lieutenant-Colonel Eduard Gorkovenko. (Artwork by David Bocquelet)

T-80BV '187' was the tank of 3rd Platoon Leader of 8th Tank Company, 3rd Tank Battalion, 6th Guards Tank Regiment. The Company, commanded by Captain Igor Vechkanov and the Tank Battalion, were assigned to 81st Guards Motor Rifle Regiment. The 187 tank developed technical difficulties on the way to loading on railway platforms on 13 November 1994. The tank was fixed and joined the main force leaving for Mozdok. Later, the tank entered Grozny with 8th Company and 81st Regiment. The tanks of 8th Company had numeration running from 180 for Company CO to 189, the first digit was not used. In addition, there were tanks bearing different numbers like '715', most probably coming from other units like 169th Tank Regiment (m/u 65347). (Artwork by David Bocquelet)

T-72A '514' tank with KMT-7 mine-roller of 1st Company, 141st Separate Tank Battalion (m/u 64514) reporting to 693rd Motor Rifle Regiment of Vladikavkaz Group. The Group included 34 tanks – a company of T-72B1 tanks of 693rd MRR and one company of T-72A tanks of 141st Separate Tank Battalion, a company of T-72B1 from 503rd MRR. The tanks of 141st Battalion were painted with white definition stripes over the single tone camouflage. 141st Battalion was one of the two units operating older T-72A tanks without ERA (the other with 9th STB of 131st Separate Motor Rifle Brigade). It took part in the fighting near Oktyabr'skoe on 28 December 1994, losing one tank to ATGM with Tank Commander, Lieutenant Nikolai Rostovsky was killed. It is not clear whether the tank numbers were sequential or loose as both the crews and hardware were picked from different companies. (Artwork by David Bocquelet)

T-80B '538' of the 2nd Company, commanded by Dmitry Zevakin, 133rd Separate Tank Battalion (m/u 52800) which took part in the fight for Khankala on 28 December 1994. 133rd Battalion, commanded by Igor Turchenyuk, had a mixture of T-80B/BV tanks and one commanders' T-80K. In December 1994, the tanks of 133rd Battalion were numbered in an odd way – 51x for the 1st Company, 53x for the 2nd Company and 55x–56x for the 3rd Company, whilst at least eight tanks of the Battalion were received from the storage depots of 83rd Separate Tank Battalion with numbers 11x and 21x. The numbering was rearranged in a more appropriate way by the end of January 1995. All T-80BV tanks were in standard 3-tone camouflage and T-80B were in an ad-hoc camouflage – some in single tone and some in improvised 3-tone. (Artwork by David Bocquelet)

R-145BM '003' was the personal mount of 131st Separate Motor Rifle Brigade Commander, Colonel Ivan Savin. The vehicle was in standard command and control configuration and manned by a team of eight including Colonel Ivan Savin and 131st Brigade Operations Officer, Lieutenant-Colonel Yury Klaptsov. The BTR crew was commanded by Lieutenant Alexey Kirilin, Platoon Leader of Signalling Battalion. At about 14:00, 31 December 1994, the BTW was hit by RPG on the left engine, near the railway station with no casualties. The crew and brigade commanders took cover under the vehicle and operated R-105 portable radio stations under the cover of brigade armour. Two hours later, at around 16:00, the BTR received another RPG round that started a fire and destroyed it completely. By that time, Colonel Savin and the team were in the building of the railway station. (Artwork by David Bocquelet)

BMP-2 '018' of Reconnaissance Company (CO Captain Oleg Tyrtyshny – callsign 'Gorets 32'), 131st Separate Motor Rifle Brigade. The Company had only three BMPs with the numbers 012, 015 and 018. BMP '018' was commanded by 4th Observation Platoon Leader, Lieutenant Arvid Kalnin, callsign 'Havana'. During the assault, the '018' was hit several times but managed to cross Sunzha River and reach positions of 276th Motor Rifle Regiment. The '012' BMP was commanded by Lieutenant Valery Danilov, callsign 'Olympus 12'. All BMPs of 131st Brigade bore single tone camouflage with Russian Federation flag painted on the turret. (Artwork by David Bocquelet)

Despite being obsolete, many units of Airborne Corps and Internal Troops operated BMD-1 vehicles. This example is from one of the Airborne Corps joint battalions having the single tone camouflage whilst the numbers and tactical signs were applied to the rear fenders. Some vehicles had white stripes applied to the front. By December 1994, the armou,r of the Airborne Corps was coming from the various units and there were no streamlined enumerations across the battalions. Like in many other cases this BMD-1 is fitted with logs that had dual purpose – giving extra protection against small arms and having on-hand material to recover the mired vehicles. It is worth mentioning that unlike motor rifle and tank units, Airborne Corps detachments did not have any kind of recovery hardware, solely depending on the manpower and ad-hoc solutions. (Artwork by David Bocquelet)

A very limited amount of 2S9 Nona self-propelled artillery took place during the early days of Russian operation in Chechnya. The most notable action was the case of a fight around Dolinsky on 12 December 1994 which was the first major engagement of the war. During the fight, a battery of Nona vehicles of 1182nd Artillery Regiment suppressed the fire of Chechen BM-21 Grad rocket launchers. 2S9 Nona vehicles were painted in standard 3-colour camouflage with numbers and tactical signs on the rear fenders, whilst on some vehicle the numbers were applied on the sides. Like the other armour of Airborne Corps, Nona SPA had logs fixed to the sides to give extra protection. (Artwork by David Bocquelet)

Russian Federation PT-76 light tank of Mechanised Company, commanded by Sergey Golubev, of 8th Separate Operational Brigade of North Caucasian Department of Ministry of Interior. PT-76 tanks of the Brigade entered Chechnya with the Group of General Rokhlin. Later, they took part in the fighting in Grozny, February – March 1995. During the assault of Bamut on 18 April 1995, Lieutenant Golubev covered the infantry that became trapped under heavy fire, with his tank. The tank was hit by several RPGs and destroyed. After the war, Mechanised Company was transferred to the newly formed 93rd Mechanised Regiment of 100th Operational Division of Internal Troops. The tanks used in 1994 and early 1995, were painted in two tone camouflage having an Internal Troops emblem, the North Caucasian Military District of Ministry of Interior emblem (insert) and no visible numbers. (Artwork by David Bocquelet)

BTR-70 '309' of the 129th Motor Rifle Regiment that was originally planned for peacekeeping operations and was part of 45th Guards Motor Rifle Division of Leningrad Military District. The Regiment operated BTR-70s and had no tank battalion. When the units were committed to the operation in Chechnya, the BTRs were the only armour assets and there was no time to reapply the regular camouflage, thus the 129th Regiment BTRs bore the Peacekeeping markings, including yellow and blue roundels with the letters MC – Russian for Peacekeeping Forces. The first combat of 129th MRR was the fight for Khankala on 28 December 1994 that resulted in the destruction of Chechen forces at a cost of seven KIA and 13 WIA, two BTRs were also destroyed. (Artwork by David Bocquelet)

MT-LBu based R-381T1 vehicle of signalling reconnaissance complex Taran used in both Chechen wars. Developed in the early 1970s and accepted by the Soviet Army in 1980, it has been used in Afghanistan since 1985. It could intercept and pinpoint enemy transmitters at a distance of up to 40km. In December 1994, the first Tactical Group of Radio Reconnaissance was deployed which included two Taran vehicles – R-381T1 and R-381T2, in Vladikavkaz with 1077th Battalion of Electronic Warfare, and in Mozdok – 1919th Battalion of EW and Navigation. The complex was used to intercept Chechen transmitters and guide Mi-8PPA/MTPP for jamming or direct aviation or artillery strikes. Later, the amount of Taran vehicles was increased with the growth of the number of EW units. No specific markings were spotted on the vehicles. (Artwork by David Bocquelet)

This 2K22 Tunguska '606' belonged to the anti-aircraft battalion of 131st Separate Motor Rifle Brigade. The battalion was split between the 131st Brigade and 81st Motor Rifle Regiment. Tunguska provided great firepower and versatility, especially against Chechen strongholds located on higher sections of buildings. On the other side, there was insufficient protection against anti-tank weapons and poor crew training including vehicle commanders and officers – some of whom never had a chance to perform a live firing exercise. The 2K22 of the 131st Brigade had single tone camouflage with the Russian Federation flag painted in the front hull and the tactical sign of the battalion. The numbers ran in 6xx range. (Artwork by David Bocquelet)

122mm 2S1 Gvozdika was a major artillery asset of the motor rifle regiments. Each regiment had an artillery battalion that normally, was split into three sections (batteries) of self-propelled with 2S1 Gvozdika, rocket artillery with BM-21 Grad and fixed with D-30 howitzers or heavy mortars. The cooperation between artillery and forward moving units was critical and eventually, artillery played one of the major roles during the Chechen campaign and in the Battle of Grozny particularly. Many Russian artillery units had very poor skills and could not provide effective cover, although in some cases, the units were outstandingly trained and proved to be very efficient. In this case, the 2S1 '313' belonged to General Rokhlin troops deployed around Tolstoi Yurt. The vehicle was of single tone camouflage with the Russian Federation flag painted on the front hull. (Artwork by David Bocquelet)

This UR-77 '901' was a part of the so-called Obstacle Breeching Detachment of 1st Guards Engineer-Sapper Brigade (Moscow Military District), including three BTR-80, four IMR-2 and three UR-77, assigned to 81st Guards Motor Rifle Regiment. UR-77 did not have a chance to show its powers in the early stage of the war – not even during the New Year assault, whilst all the vehicles were destroyed. Later, it was used efficiently to overcome Chechen defences during street fighting in Grozny and in other parts of Chechnya. The UR-77 remained one of the rare armoured vehicles to be spotted in the Chechen campaign. The vehicles were painted in single tone camouflage with Russian Federation flags and tactical numbers. (Artwork by David Bocquelet)

BTS and BREM were the most common recovery assets in the Russian motor rifle regiments. During the first days of the Chechen campaign, the vehicles were used not only for recovery but for breaching the numerous barricades set-up by locals on the routes of the Russian advance. Ironically, BTS as a non-fighting vehicle, was employed on several occasions to scare the local protesters in Ingushetia with a loud engine roar and smoke screen, running back and forth over the road. As was the common case with engineering vehicles – no specific markings besides the numbers were applied, like in this example of BTS-4A '904'. (Artwork by David Bocquelet)

A MiG-17F jet of Grozny Aviation Training Centre (GATC) of DOSAAF – Volunteer Society for Cooperation with the Army, Aviation and Navy. The Centre was established in 1960 and started training operations in 1963, using the airfield at Kalinovskaya, operating MiG-15UTI and MiG-17F. After the collapse of the Soviet Union, the GATC was disbanded and Drozhokhar Dudaev took over the remaining assets, whilst most of the jets were already scrapped and only several remained in serviceable condition – three MiG-17F, two MiG-15UTI and two Mi-8T. The condition of the jets rapidly deteriorated as there was absolutely no spare parts and there was only one MiG-17F seen flying by mid-1993, probably grounded by the end of the year. All GATC aircraft were destroyed on the ground during the Russian attacks of Kalinovskaya in November – December 1994. GATC jets had the same colour as other Soviet aircraft whilst it could be with or without DOSAAF markings (word 'ДОСААФ' in red) applied. (Artwork by Tom Cooper)

The most numerous aircraft of the Air Forces of Ichkeria were L-29 Dolphins, inherited from 382nd Training Aviation Regiment. The scores of jets were impressively lined up in Khankala airfield but never went into the air. By the 1991, when Stavropol Stavropol High Military Aviation College of Pilots and Navigators stopped its operations in Grozny, those jets were already obsolete, lacking spares and had not received proper maintenance. According to some rumours, Chechens managed to get one L-29 into flying condition and even applied an Ichkeria paint scheme, but there is no evidence of such aircraft ever existing. Nevertheless, the reports about Dzhokhar Dudaev's ambitious plans to get hundreds of attack aircraft into the air and attack Russian targets, creating havoc in the country, spooked the minds of Russian military planners and triggered massive airstrike on the airfields in Grozny, Khankala and Kalinovskaya. All L-29s remained in original Soviet markings. (Artwork by Tom Cooper)

The best-known aircraft operated by Dzhokhar Dudaev's forces was the L-39 Albatross that came from the assets of the 382nd Training Aviation Regiment of Stavropol High Military Aviation College of Pilots and Navigators, based in Khankala and was the first unit to operate L-39 in 1974. It is believed that only six jets were maintained in flying condition. Probably, this was the amount of aircraft that received Air Force of Ichkeria markings: all the other aircraft lacked the same. Chechen L-39s flew several missions against opposition forces, dropping improvised munitions like tanks with gasoline, with limited, if any, results. One jet was downed in Urus Martan district on 3 October 1994, with two pilots killed. All L-39 jets were destroyed on the ground during Russian air strikes. (Artwork by Tom Cooper)

Despite Moscow's attempts to remove all the serviceable aircraft out of Chechnya, at least two operational Mi-8Ts were left in the territory. These included the example – the reconstruction of which is shown here, Bort number 'Yellow 39' and the Bort number 'Red 23'. Both retained their camouflage pattern as at the time of the take-over, but subsequently received the national insignia, in form of a large crest of the Ichkerian Republic, in black and white, although with a row of five-pointed stars at the bottom (applied in yellow, instead of nine-pointed stars applied in white, as official). Moscow-supported Chechen oppositional forces operated a number of Mi-8MTs in 1994, but these wore no national markings at all and were flown by Russian crews. (Artwork by Tom Cooper)

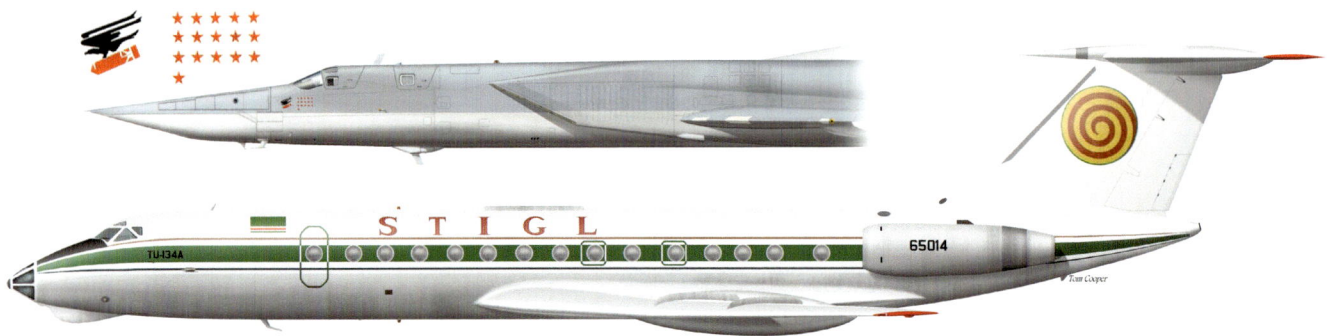

Tu-134A-3 'CCCP-65014' was one of seven aircraft operated by the Chechen national carrier STIGL ('Sky' in Chechen language), established in 1992 from the Grozny Aviation Detachment. Unofficially, this airliner was the personal aircraft of Dzhokhar Dudaev which he used to fly personally. Whilst STIGL was not officially registered in Russia, it used to operate to Turkey and Arab countries, as a VIP carrier and airliner, ignored by the Russian authorities – even when flying to Moscow Vnukovo, in July 1994. All but two of the airliners were destroyed in the Russian airstrike on Grozny-Severny, on 25 November 1994: one ended up in Khartoum, and another was flown to Ingushetia. Insert shows the front part of one of Tu-22M-3 bombers of the 326th Heavy Bomber Aviation Division, commanded by Dudaev from 1987 until 1991. (Artwork by Tom Cooper)

An-2R 'CCCP-71263' was operated by Grozny United Aviation Detachment (82nd Detachment) of the North Caucasian Directorate of Civil Aviation from 1984. The first An-2T was delivered to Grozny Detachment in 1954 and by 1985, there were 34 An-2 mostly of R type. By the time Dzhokhar Dudaev took over power in Chechnya, there were seven An-2 aircraft in flying condition. They remained in the AEROFLOT colours and performed liaison and transport duties, whilst one was downed by opposition forces in September 1993, with the loss of the crew. There were claims that An-2s were bombing the settlements under opposition control, but no evidence was ever provided. In late November 1994, all An-2s were destroyed or damaged during Russian airstrikes. (Artwork by Tom Cooper)

In summer 1994, Chechen opposition forces, led by Umar Avturkhanov, started to receive a constantly increasing support of weapons from Russia. This also included aviation assets that comprised several Mi-8 and Mi-24 helicopters, piloted by Russian crews. Mi-8 were used for transport missions but were mostly grounded due to poor technical conditions, as was the case of Mi-24. The details of the operations are nonexistent but it was reported that several attacks on Dudaev's forces were performed and there was one recorded loss of Mi-24 gunship. The most known appearance of opposition aviation was shortly before the ill-fated assault on Grozny, 26 November 1994, by when they wore no insignia at all. The fate of the helicopters in question remains unknown but it is assumed that they were re-integrated into the Russian armed forces. (Artwork by Tom Cooper)

Su-25 red '39' of 2nd Squadron of 899th Separate Attack Aviation Regiment (m/u 10135) commanded by Colonel Alexander Golovin. The group of squadron size with 12 Su-25 and two Su-25UB, was based in Mozdok and started operations from 9 December 1994. On 13 December, Su-25UB was damaged by 23mm anti-aircraft fire over Novy-Sharoi, resulting in engine shutdown. The crew of Major Andrey Vakhovsky and Major Yury Talalaev, managed to get back to Mozdok and successfully landed. The Regiment was newly formed in July 1993 as 899th Fighter-Attack Aviation Regiment (inheriting the number from one of the oldest Russian aviation units – 899th Aviation Regiment of Fighter-Bombers, disbanded 24 August 1992), fully based on the disbanded 186th Fighter-Attack Aviation Regiment (ex-Borisoglebsk High Military Aviation College, m/u 21513), reporting to 1080th Training Aviation Centre. In December 1993, it was reassigned to 16th Air Army and became 899th Separate Attack Aviation Regiment. (Artwork by Tom Cooper)

Mi-8T No. 27 (Red '27') of 325th Separate Helicopter Regiment (m/u 62978) was hit by small arms and performed an emergency landing near Novy Sharoy on 14 December 1994. The helicopter was leading a pair of Mi-8s with supplies for the elements of 76th Airborne Division of Vladikavkaz Group and was escorted by a pair of Mi-24 gunships of 55th Separate Helicopter Regiment. The commander of the Mi-8 pair made a navigational mistake and flew over a highly defended area, eventually coming under heavy anti-aircraft fire. The crew of the downed helicopter included Lieutenant-Colonel Nikolai Leskov, Captain Nikolai Malkov and Senior Lieutenant Sergey Devyatkov, who were all killed by the Chechens. This was the first loss of Russian aviation during the war. (Artwork by Tom Cooper)

A map of the Republic of Ichkeria, with neighbouring members of the Russian Federation and (south) northern Georgia. (Map by George Anderson)

Opposition preparations for the 26 November assault – BTR-60 with ZU-23-2 (left), T-72A tank (middle) and BTR-80 (right). Note, all vehicles bear no markings. (Efim Sandler collection)

opposition commanders. Another armour asset included about 40 BTR-80s and a couple of R-145BMs. The overall control should be managed by General Kolesnikov and his staff onboard a Mi-9 helicopter.

The teams and crews had never trained together, commanders did not know each other and there was no common understanding of the plan. The only communication means were 80 R-105M portable radio packs that were phased out from the Soviet military in the 1980s. The intelligence that supposedly had to be provided by Grozny locals, was nonexistent. Colonel Akhmed Kelimatov, responsible for leading the main force, offered the group commanders a visit to Grozny a couple of days before the operation to walk the route of advance – nothing was ever done. The only units that made a decent reconnaissance were two Special Force teams – they made it all the way to the President's Palace and back, checking the routes and making notes of Dudaev's forces.

Their reports were more than alarming – it seemed the whole plan was compromised – the routes of advance were packed by Dudaev's forces blocking positions and with ambush teams. Special Force men suggested that armour group commanders should consider alternative routes but this was overruled by superiors. On the eve of the operation, Russian crews were instructed not to show themselves out of tanks and to use fake Chechen names. The tanks were also painted with white colour applied to some spots.

During the night of 25–26 November, the forces concentrated in Tolstoy-Yurt, included five infantry battalions commanded by Gerikhanov, Satuev, Tulanov, Khambulatov and Saidov. The group of Ruslan Labazanov's could hardly be named 'a battalion' as it consisted of about 25 members, there was also a group of Chechen Ministry of Interior members led by Khamid Inalov and a battalion of Beslan Gantemirov. The tanks arrived but many were very low on fuel despite the promises of Russian commanders. The plan of operation was ruined from the very beginning – instead of heading to Grozny at 04:30, by sunrise, the opposition forces were still trying to manage the tank fuel issue and then gather everybody together. Meanwhile, the Special Forces detachments made their way to the Palace and fired several RPO-A rounds, waiting for the armour to show up at 06:00 – nothing happened. By 09:00, the convoy just managed to enter Grozny and bypass the Cannery Plant. At this point, the opposition units came under constant sniper fire from the roofs along the route – Yahya Gerikhanov and several other commanders were killed or badly wounded.

Moving over Mayakovsky Street towards the Printing House, Umar Avturkhanov ordered to stop and used the R-145BM to talk to Mozdok. Gantemirov tried to connect to his men but with no success. By 11:00, communications with all units were totally lost. The majority of units reached their objectives but were encircled by numerous groups of Dudaev's forces. The promised units of Grozny locals never materialised and it looked like a fake promise by Umar Avturkhanov. The leading T-72 tanks with Russian crews, remained alone as the infantry disappeared – they moved from junction to junction, stopping and asking people for directions. The crews tried to call their superiors but it seemed that the radios were out of range and they never got any response. Finally, the tanks reached their respective objectives while five of them positioned around the President's Palace – this was a trap. Chechen militants, commanded by Aslan Maskhadov, used a classical ambush scheme – firing from the roof tops of toll buildings and from the cellars.

The core of Maskhadov defences was combined of three units numbering 50–100 men each – RDB of Shamil Basaev, Borz of Khamsat (Ruslan) Gelaev and the President's Guard, led by Abu Arsanukaev. In total there were a little over 200 men, reinforced by several ad-hoc territorial units of small size. The plan worked well and Maskhadov's men attacked from numerous directions knocking out a dozen of tanks and BTRs in a matter of minutes, causing great panic. The opposition forces who were trying to retreat the same way as they had moved in, found themselves blocked under constant fire.

Then came the tanks. Further, to a person who is far from both tactics and strategy, it is clear that tanks cannot be driven into the narrow streets of the city. This can only be called idiocy. The tanks clanged their tracks, rolled their barrels around and sometimes fired, apparently into nowhere: no explosions from shells could be seen through our small window. The tanks were moving in a column of five vehicles. Suddenly there was an explosion, sparks flew like from a Bengal fire, and viscous, black smoke poured out – a grenade from an RPG-7, fired by one of the Chechen militias, hit the front car exactly where the tower connects to the hull.

A hatch opened in the wrecked tank, and a smoking fighter in black overalls literally rolled out. Suddenly, a dark figure separated from the wall of the house, ran up to the tankman, grabbed him by the collar, and dragged him to the nearest yard. And just in time: ammunition exploded in a burning tank, its turret was torn off and, spinning a couple of times in the air, threw it at the nearest kiosk.

The rest of the tanks found themselves in a difficult situation: after standing like a herd of mastodons contemplating the death of their comrade in bewilderment, they moved back in hysterics – in reverse, of course, sweeping away cars and telephone booths parked at the side of the road, since the general picture of the battle was as follows: tanks broke into the city, lagging behind the infantry, which, in fact, should run from behind, hiding behind armour and destroying enemy grenade launchers.

The defenders immediately took advantage of this oversight because it is not difficult to shoot cars with people in narrow

The turrets of destroyed Russian T-72A tanks serving as decorations in the center of Grozny. (Photo by Ivan Shlamov)

streets from the windows of houses. Then began the 'beating' of armoured vehicles.

In a city without infantry support, tanks are almost as helpless as a lion caught in a trap. Some tankers, without waiting for the terrible outcome, simply left their completely undamaged vehicles and tried to hide. They were caught. Those who resisted were shot on the spot, the rest were taken hostages to the basements.

Meanwhile at 14:00, based on a message from Umar Avturkhanov, the Russian TASS media agency reported that Grozny was taken by the opposition forces and the power had switched to a new government. During the day, Russian news channels made several reports of fighting in Grozny and spotted armoured convoys. In the early afternoon, Chechen sources reported Russians manning tanks, probably taking the first prisoners or getting information from opposition sources.

The commanders of the North-Caucasian Military District promptly dismissed any information of Russian forces involved in fighting. At the same time, the opposition forces started to leave the city under constant sniper fire. Tank crews found themselves in a totally unfamiliar city with no supporters – one-by-one, the tanks were lit up or abandoned. The fighting continued till late afternoon as the opposition team, led by Khelimatov, managed to take and hold the Publishing House with four tanks later joining them. By night, it was decided to escape the city with tanks leading, followed by the car of Avturkhanov, remaining BTRs and other vehicles moving over Mayakovsky Street towards the Cannery Plant and out. At 22:00, the convoy reached Tolstoy-Yurt – it was all over. The operation failed.

The result was devastating; according to Chechen sources, 200 opposition forces were killed, about 100 taken prisoners, including at least 31 Russian servicemen. Opposition sources mentioned 115 killed, probably not including Russians. From all the tanks, only four managed to leave the city. Chechen militants and civilian losses have never been known but Zelimkhan Yandarbiev mentioned that defenders suffered significant losses, especially State Security of Ichkeria (i.e., Chechnya). Dudaev's propaganda machine worked perfectly – all channels around the world were showing the results of the assault with still smoking tanks and captured Russian soldiers. The Minister of Defence, Pavel Grachev, publicly denied any participation of Russian servicemen in the fighting calling his men 'mercenaries'.

The next two weeks became known as the PoW crisis: following the Herculean efforts of several Russian parliamentary missions and later the Ministry of Defence, 18 Russian servicemen were released and the three bodies of Russian tankmen killed in action, were transferred by the Chechens. It was known that at least one officer was executed by the Chechen DGB – Department of State Security. By then, it was still unclear how many Russians were taken hostage and how many were killed – this would be the bitter truth of the upcoming war.

Controversies

There were several controversial moments that never received any clarification. The fact that the assault plan was compromised is supported by all sources but the question remains – why and who provided Dudaev with the information? On one hand, the simple explanation was that the routes and maps were leaked from the opposition commanders – this version is pretty solid but there were only a very limited number of people exposed to the whole plan, and none of them could be considered as a potential Dudaev agent, even for money. Another version is that there was a so-called '3rd

Captured Russian tankmen during the press-conference in the President's Palace in Grozny on 30 November 1994. At least 31 Russian servicemen were killed or taken prisoners. (Photo by Misha Japaridze)

Chechen T-72A tanks of Shali Tank Regiment pictured in early December 1994. Note, the turret is already painted in white, anticipating the Russian advance. (Author's collection)

when they started to receive sniper fire.

On paper, the plan included advancing over four directions, however, only three advanced as Ruslan Labazanov brought only 25 men with him and carry out much action (or did not plan to carry out much). Belsan Gantemirov left his force and joined Avturkhanov, whilst without a leader, his men just took the positions in one of the military compounds and never moved further. There was no explanation behind Gantemirov's acts but many thought he would like to be close to the victory rather focusing on his objectives.

Another question is about the involvement of other forces such as aviation. There is a commonly circulated rumour that on 23 November, Russian aviation attacked compartments of Shali Tank Regiment destroying about 20 tanks – half of its force – thus preventing it from defending Grozny. This is very unlikely. First, there is no evidence of such an attack via foreign media channels like APF or Reuters that were very active to cover developments in Chechnya, as well as from Chechen sources. The fact that the Shali Tank Regiment strength was about half of its nominal number is explanatory – about half of the tanks left by Russians were in unserviceable condition. The major reason for the Regiment tanks not taking part in defence of Grozny was that its commanders disputed Dudaev orders. Nevertheless, it seems some tanks were positioned in Grozny and were credited with destruction of one to two opposition tanks – this is highly tentative as no clear accounts or evidence exist.

Force' in Moscow that provided Chechens with the information. Why this force was not interested in overthrowing Dudaev, can only be guessed, but some people at the very top levels were not ready to stop the hostilities. In contrast, they wanted a full-blown war with Chechnya. This was probably the same force that did not allow Ruslan Khasbulatov to continue with the peace process and attempt to prepare a compromise between nationalists and Russian authorities.

The number and quality of the opposition forces could never be determined precisely. What can be said for sure is that there were 35 (or 36) T-72A tanks and several dozens of APCs – all BTRs of several types. The reports of Russian self-propelled artillery (SPA) and self-propelled anti-aircraft weapons were mere fantasies. Opposition artillery that entered Grozny included several towed D-30 howitzers and GAZ-66 trucks with ZU-23-2 installed, none of the SPA or SPAAA were ever provided by Russians. The numbers vary from 1,500 to 4,500 men but it seems there were hardly more than 2,000 men, mostly in Umar Avturkhanov's forces and only a handful reached the centre, as most of the infantry left the tanks

Clearly, the major factors of failure were non-acceptance of the incoming intelligence by the decision makers, almost non-existing cooperation between infantry and tanks, along with the inability to control combined arms operations in the urban environment. Despite all this, the situation was presented differently.

Later, Chechen opposition leaders tried to explain the failure as a matter of sabotage. For example, Beslan Gantemirov, in his interview talked about tanks that were mined and exploded from inside. Others mentioned tank rounds that were not firing or exploded in the barrels. No-one though, accused the Russian military authorities and FSB, of absolute incompetence in planning and execution, plus obvious leakage of information.

The Russian Minister of Defence, Pavel Grachev, in his interview following the events, on 28 November 1994 said the words that proved to be a 'black' prophecy: 'If that would be a Russian army, I would never allow to push tanks into the city, as it would be a total ignorance. Moreover, with just one paratrooper regiment, we could solve all the issues.'

The only person who took the issue personally was the Commander of 4th Kantemirov Division, General Boris Polyakov – he voluntarily resigned from his position and left the Army.

9
BUILDING THE FORCE

After the failed assault on Grozny of 26 November, it became obvious to Moscow that the one and only solution would be to take it with brutal force. The only thing missing was the cause for attack; this appeared within less than 48 hours. On 28 November, Vice President Chernomyrdin initiated the so-called, 'appeal of Caucasian people to the President to protect human rights and law'. Following this letter, President Yeltsin issued an ultimatum for illegal entities of Chechnya to hand over their weapons. The ultimatum was understood by Dudaev in exactly the opposite fashion, and thus only poured more oil on the fire.

On the next day, there was a closed Security Council meeting that some members called 'Yeltsin's private party'. No protocol was ever recorded and the one and only issue was the incoming pacifying operation in Chechnya. Grachev demanded more reasoning as Chechen resistance could be tougher than expected. On the other side, Egorov and Chernomyrdin insisted that the majority of the Chechen population would greet incoming Russian troops and accused Grachev of not receiving the proper information and being passive. Moreover, Victor Chernomyrdin moved so far as openly demanding the Minister of Defence resign due to his incompetence. Eventually, Boris Yeltsin decided to agree with with Grachev but ordered him to move in and take over Chechnya.

In accordance with President Boris Yeltsin's directive of 30 November 1994, No. 2137c – Actions of Restoring Constitutional Order and Law in Republic of Chechnya, Armed Forces of the Ministry of Defence, Ministry of Interior and FSB, were tasked with taking the situation under control and disarming Dudaev's supporters. Immediately, General HQ issued an Order No. 312/1/00143sh of planning and executing the special operations by combined armed forces.

Eventually the operation received the attention of General HQ and in October 1994, Yeltsin asked Grachev to work out possible scenarios for military actions in Chechnya, including a joint forces operation of the Ministry of Defence, Ministry of Interior and FSB. Pavel Grachev ordered to set-up a working group of HQ officers, headed by First Deputy of Chief of Operations, General Anatoly Kvashnin and Deputy of Chief of Operations, General Leonty Shevtsov.

The operation was planned to have four stages and would be concluded in 3 weeks.

First: 30 November to 6 December – to create the Joint Group of Forces of Ministry of Defence and Ministry of Interior and move the units to the forward positions upon relevant directions. All involved attack and support aviation elements which would be deployed at the forward airfields by 1 December.

Second: 7–9 December – move towards Grozny under close air support and block the city. The units of the Ministry of Defence supported by Internal Troops, would push over six directions towards Grozny and set-up an inner security circle upon the city boundaries. The outer security circle would be set by Border Guards and elements of the Ministry of Interior over the republic perimeter.

Third: 10–13 December – with Ministry of Defence, units would take control over key infrastructure objectives in Grozny, including the President's Palace, Supreme Council, television, radio, et cetera, disarm the members of illegal organisations and requisite armour and other heavy weapons.

Fourth: 14–21 December – stabilise the situation and transfer the responsibility to the elements of the Ministry of Interior. The Special Forces of FSB and Ministry of Interior would be ready to pinpoint and neutralise potentially hostile elements capable of armed sabotage and terrorist actions against Russian troops.

The working group to manage the operation was headed by the Minister of Defence, Pavel Grachev, and included:

- N. Egorov – Minister of Nationalities Affairs
- V. Yerin – Minister of Internal Affairs
- A. Kruglov – Chairman of Customs Committee
- A. Kulikov – Deputy Minister of Internal Affairs
- A. Nikolaev – Commander of Border Guarding troops
- V. Panichev – Chief Military Prosecutor
- B. Pastukhov – Deputy of Minister of Foreign Affairs
- A. Starovoytov – Chief of Federal Information and Communications Agency
- S. Stepashin – Director of Federal Service of Counter-Intelligence (FSB)
- P. Shirshov – Chairman of Defence and Security Committee of Federation Council
- S. Yushenkov – Chairman of Defence Committee of State Duma

The next issue was to form the Command of Joint Group of Forces and this proved to be complicated. The best candidate for the job was General Boris Gromov – a decorated veteran of Soviet-Afghan war where he topped as a Commander 40th Army and later, became a Deputy of Minister of Defence. Boris Gromov was the only one who openly opposed the invasion of Chechnya and was sent for retirement. The next in line was General Eduard Vorobyov, who commanded Russian troops in Moldova and Tajikistan but in turn, Vorobyov declined and submitted his resignation (eventually Grachev insisted on a court-marshal but was overruled by Yeltsin).

Pavel Grachev was desperate and tried to appoint General Alexander Chindarov, Deputy Commander of Airborne Corps, but this appointment did not go well. Finally, the one who took the role, was General Alexey Mityukhin, Commander of North-Caucasian Military District. Mityukhin, spent 17 years in commanding positions in the Group of Soviet Forces in Germany (GSVG), having no combat experience and being in total disagreement with operation management at the top level, remained an officer who do not question orders.

Initially, the Joint Group of Forces was planned to include following units;

- Brigade size detachment of 20th Motor-Rifle Division, VIII Army Corps
- Brigade size detachment of 19th Motor-Rifle Division, XLII Army Corps
- 131st Separate Motor-Rifle Brigade, LXVII Army Corps
- Joint regiment of 76th Airborne Division
- Joint regiment of 106th Airborne Division
- Elements of 21st and 56th Separate Airborne Assault Brigades
- Elements of Internal Troops of Ministry of Interior
- Strike and Attack aviation of 4th Air Army

In total, at least on paper, there were about 15,000 personnel, 158 tanks, 346 BMD and BMP, 421 BTR and BTR-D, 148 artillery pieces, 121 anti-tank systems, 61 anti-aircraft defence systems, 85 helicopters and about 2,500 soft-skin vehicles.

On paper, the Joint Group was a formidable unit but in reality, it was a mixture of underpowered and incompetent units that had never trained together. The essence of the term 'joint unit' meant that the unit was combined from everybody available in its parent unit, no matter what military profession or experience –cooks could find themselves as tank drivers or infantry RPG operators. The higher level of units as company and battalions were never trained together and their respective commanders mainly saw each other just before the operation. For example, for the Airborne Corps, the order to provide three joint regiments and two joint battalions and transport them to Mozdok, came on 29 November 1994.

Besides all the other issues experienced by the Russian military in the early1990s, this was the worst time due to the rotation of the personnel – seasoned soldiers were discharged and sent home and new recruits were replacing them. This would cause problems later as some units had about 40 percent fresh recruits who were unfamiliar with their duties, weapons and discipline.

Nevertheless, in 72 hours, Airborne Corps flew two regiments to Mozdok (one from 76th and another from 106th Division), joint battalion of 56th Brigade marched from Volgodonsk (750km) and another battalion of 21st Brigade, marched from Stavropol (400km), followed by the newly formed 45th Special Forces Regiment that arrived on 2 December. By 3 December, Airborne Corps Group numbered 4,320 men.

According to reports, the level of equipment of the Ministry of Defence units was at the level of 60 percent, the Ministry of Interior – 70 percent and militia/OMON – 45 percent. The majority of the vehicles were at 80 percent life-limit while 10 percent were totally unusable. In order to seal the gap in equipment, the Ministry of Defence ordered various units to 'contribute/donate' the vehicles. This process had an even more devastating outcome –the vehicles were simply junk. For example, the party sent by Volga Military District included about 40 percent of unserviceable BTRs and out of 18 howitzers, calibre .122mm, only six were operational.

The same was valid for the Ural Military District: only four out of 18 artillery systems delivered could be used and the situation was similar in regards of BTRs. Aviation readiness was about 60 percent while the average annual army aviation pilot training, mounted about 40–50 hours at the most. The low visibility, bad weather and night conditions were not accounted for at all.

Another issue was manpower. The average headcount of Russian forces before the operation stood at an average of 64 percent while some units were as low as 30 percent. About 90 percent of professional officers left the military during the early 1990s and were replaced by newcomers and the so-called '2-years', aka officers who received military training as part of their technical degree in college, taking part in 1–2 months field training. They were contracted for either one year as an NCO or two years as officers. Needless to say, those platoon leaders who never saw their platoon members and never trained in joint combat environment, could hardly manage their units.

Another issue was poor supplies in terms of food and apparel – at the beginning of the operation in Chechnya, Russian units had about 65 percent of food supplies. Being ripped of money, thanks to the 'reforms' led by V. Chernomyrdin and A. Chubais, the military could not pay for supplies and had to earn its food working on private farms or selling its assets to private business. Even 'elite' Airborne Corps companies had about 60–70 percent of manpower and 50–60 percent of equipment, while about 70 percent of the professional officers with the real combat experience, left the Corps in 1993–94.

One of numerous examples can be seen in 131st Maikop Separate Motor-Rifle Brigade. The Brigade was manned and equipped under the 'peace-time condition'. In total, there were 1,282 men including 207 officers, 53 NCOs and 1,022 soldiers. One reduced tank battalion with only 28 T-72A tanks, two reduced motor-rifle battalions with 48 BMP-2, eight BTRs, and 208 soft-skin vehicles. The majority of vehicles were in poor technical condition and demanded serious attention by maintenance teams. In the

BMD-2 vehicles of Russian Airborne Corps unit, probably of 76th Airborne Division, based in Beslan, pictured on 3 December 1994 (Photo by Alexander Zamlianichenko)

tank battalion only one, 3rd Company, was fully equipped with tanks and crews, two others were filled 'on the fly' from different units – for example several men of 152nd Tank Regiment (military unit 44688) of 27th Motor-Rifle Division arrived on 5 December 1994 and were assigned to 1st Company. Many officers held several positions besides their primary job including filling in for missing crewmembers such as gunners.

Every crew received only one piece of weapon – AKS-74/74U that was assigned to the gunner. The situation in motor-rifle battalions was even more alarming – instead of four battalions with 400–450 men each, there were only two with 240–250 each. Every company had just 40–50 men with five to six BMP-2s. Moreover, not every company had a Company Commander and other officer positions. Commanding officers were already assigned in Mozdok and many were not familiar with their respective units. There was a similar situation in other Brigade units – for example, the Reconnaissance Company had only three BMP-2s and 30 soldiers and officers, de facto it was a platoon size unit.

By 5 December, the Joint Group of Federal Forces had been mostly set-up, focusing on the three major directions: Mozdok, Kizlyar and Vladikavkaz. By the eve of the operation, the initial Joint Group of Federal Forces (aka JGFF) was set-up as following:

Group 1 (or Mozdok Group), commanded by General Vladimir Chilindin, and included the following joint elements:

- 131st Separate Motor-Rifle Brigade
- Battalion of 481st Rocket Anti-Aircraft Regiment, 19th Motor-Rifle Division
- Battalion of 170th Engineering-Sapper Brigade
- Detachment of 22nd Separate Special Force Brigade (173 OOSpN reinforced by 411st OOSpN)
- Detachment of 67th Separate Special Forces Brigade (691st OOSpN)
- Regiment of 106th Airborne Division (battalions of 137th and 51st Regiments)
- Battalion of 56th Separate Airborne Brigade
- Battalion of 173rd Separate Pontoon-Bridge Brigade (Engineers)
- 59th Operational Regiment of Ministry of Interior
- 81st Operational Regiment of Ministry of Interior
- 451st Operational Regiment of Ministry of Interior
- 6th Detachment of Special Forces of Ministry of Interior
- 80 helicopters (including 39 Mi-24 of 55th Separate Helicopter Regiment) based in Mozdok

In total, (at least reportedly) the Group had 6,567 personnel, 41 tanks (tank battalion of 131 SMRBr with T-72A tanks), 99 BTRs, 132 BMPs and 54 artillery pieces. However, there were numerous reports of machinery in poor or unserviceable condition but the real numbers are unknown.

Group 2 (or Vladikazkaz Group), commanded by General Aleksander Chindarov, and included the following joint elements:

- 693rd Motor-Rifle Regiment, 19th Motor-Rifle Division
- Battalion of 481st Rocket Anti-Aircraft Regiment, 19th Motor-Rifle Division
- Battalion of 933rd Rocket Anti-Aircraft Regiment, XLII Army Corps
- Regiment of 76th Airborne Division (battalions of 237th and 104th Regiments)
- Battalion of 21st Separate Airborne Brigade
- 46th Operational Regiment of Ministry of Interior
- 47th Operational Regiment of Ministry of Interior
- 7th Detachment of Special Forces of Ministry of Interior
- 14 helicopters (including eight Mi-24 of 55 Separate Helicopter Regiment) based in Beslan

In total, the Group had 3,915 personnel, 34 tanks (a company of T-72B1 tanks of 693 MRR and one company of T-72A tanks of 141 Separate Tank Battalion, a company of T-72B1 from 503 MRR), 67 BTRs, 98 BMPs and 62 artillery pieces.

Group 3 (or Kizlyar Group), commanded by General Lev Rokhlin, and included the following joint elements:

- 255th Motor-Rifle Regiment (20th Motor-Rifle Division)
- Battalion of 67th Rocket Anti-Aircraft Brigade
- Battalion of AAA from 135th Motor-Rifle Brigade
- 68th Separate Reconnaissance Battalion (20th Motor-Rifle Division)
- Battalion of 173rd Separate Pontoon-Bridge Brigade (Engineers)
- Battalion of 1st Engineering-Sapper Brigade (Moscow Military District)
- 57th Operational Regiment of Ministry of Interior
- 63rd (81st?) Operational Regiment of Ministry of Interior
- 49th Operational Regiment of Ministry of Interior
- 18 helicopters (including eight Mi-24 of 487 Separate Helicopter Regiment) based in Kizlyar

In total, the Group had 4,053 personnel, seven tanks (20th Separate Tank Battalion), 162 BTRs and 28 artillery pieces.

Six routes were planned for the deployment of Russian Joint Forces – two per each Group:

1. Mozdok – Bratskoe – Znamenskoye – Nadterechnoye – Ken-Yurt – Pervomayskoye
2. Mozdok – Predgornoe – Novy Redant – Goragorsk – Kerla-Yurt – Pervomayskaya
3. Chermen – Verhniye Achaluki – Karabulak – Sernovyudsk – Alkhan-Kala – Alkhan-Yurt
4. Chermen – Gamurgievo – North Yandyrka – Novy Sharoy – Alkhan-Yurt
5. Kizlyar – Khanamat-Yurt – Nizhny Gerzel – Gerzel-Aul – Novogroznensky
6. Terekli – Mekteb – Baklan – Lugovoye – Chervlenaya-Uzlovaya – Vinogradnaya – Petropavlovskaya (this is not the original route but a corrected one from 11 December 1994)

Air Force

The situation with the Air Force component of the Joint Group of Federal Forces was not much better than for the ground force. The reality of the economic turmoil had its direct implications. For example, the combat practice plans of 1993–94 were accomplished by 30–36 percent due to insufficient fuel supplies and the poor technical condition of the airplanes. During this time, the command of the Russian Air Force cut the training agenda for the personnel which affected most complex attributes like usage of PGMs, bad weather flying, nocturnal attacks with the aid of illuminating munitions and low level profiles. The average pilot's annual flying time was reportedly marked at 40–50 hours but in reality, it could be as low as 10 hours for some units.

Practice training was down to basic manoeuvres just to prevent possible misfortune to the aircraft. For example, the main tactical bomber of the Russian Air Force was Su-24 that was a very complex machine to fly, it had seen limited usage in Afghanistan but the majority of fresh pilots could not handle the machine beyond the basic flying profile.

Another issue was a leakage of aerial and ground personnel due to economic issues. Not receiving pay checks month after month, many pilots turned towards promising contracts around the world. The situation was even more alarming with experienced ground crew, whilst the Russian military leadership did absolutely nothing to keep people interested. Many found their ways to the private ventures in Russia and around the world.

Following the withdrawal from Eastern Europe, many units were in a process of reorganisation like elements of 4th and 16th Air Armies. For example, the 10th Bombing Aviation Division and 1st Guards Strike Aviation Division (both of 4th Army) were in the middle of transferring to new hardware. With all this, the backbone of the Russian Air Force commanders (about 60 percent) were Soviet-Afghan War veterans who could fly in all kinds of conditions and logged hundreds of hours of real combat experience. The most potent strike unit by 1993–94 was 461st Strike Aviation Regiment, flying Su-25, which was heavily involved in operations against Mujahidin in Tajik-Afghan border area.

The core of Air Force component of the Joint Group of Federal Forces looked as following:

- 461st Strike Aviation Regiment (Su-25), based in Krasnodar
- 368th Strike Aviation Regiment (Su-25), based in Budennovsk
- 899th Separate Strike Aviation Regiment (Su-25), based in Buturlinovka
- 959th Bomber Aviation Regiment (Su-24), based in Yeisk
- 559th Bomber Aviation Regiment (Su-24), based in Morozovsk
- 960th Fighter Aviation Regiment (Mig-29), based in Primorsko-Akhtarsk
- 31st Fighter Aviation Regiment (Mig-29), based in Zelenograd
- 11th Separate Reconnaissance Aviation Regiment (Su-24MR), based in Marinovka and Budennovsk
- 47th Separate Reconnaissance Aviation Regiment (Mig-25RB), based in Mozdok and Rostov
- 5th Separate Long-Range Reconnaissance Squadron of 16th Aviation Army, (An-30), based in Rostov
- 870th Heavy Bomber Aviation Regiment (Tu-22M3), based in Sol'tsy, Novgorod
- 52nd Heavy Bomber Aviation Regiment (Tu-22M3), based in Shaikovka, Kaluga
- 1225th Heavy Bomber Aviation Regiment (Tu-22M3), based in Belaya, Irkutsk

In total, there were 515 aircraft of various types including: 72 Su-24, 85 Su-25, 50 (49) Mig-29, 33 Su-24MR, 35 Mig-25RB, 14 (21) Tu-22M3. Note that all Tu-22M3 bombers operated from Engels airbase.[1]

In addition, there was an Air Defence element mostly comprised of the units of XII Separate Corps of Air Defence – 209th Guards Fighter Aviation Regiment (Su-27/Mig-23ML – in 1993 529th Regiment operating Su-27 was amalgamated with 393rd Regiment operating Mig-23MLs, under 116th Centre of Combat Application based in Astrakhan) and 562nd (Mig-31) Fighter Aviation Regiment, reinforced by elements of 786th (Mig-31) and 54th (Su-27/30) Fighter Aviation Regiments of 148th Centre of Combat Applications and Transition of Air Crews, A-50 AWACs of 144th Separate Aviation Regiment, 110th Radio-Technical Regiment (based in Astrakhan).

Special mission aircraft were provided from different units around Russia, like Mi-8PPA jammers, An-26RT communications relay, Tu-134A VIP transport, Il-22 ELINT, et cetera. Transport missions were mostly flown by units operating Il-76 carriers like 103rd, 117th and 334th Transport Aviation Regiments, whilst other transport assets included An-12, An-22 and even a mighty An-124.

Results of Russian airstrike on Grozny-Severny airport on 1 December 1994. Note, the destroyed Tu-134A 'CCCP-65014' of STIGL carrier – the airliner was the personal aircraft of Dzhokhar Dudaev. (via Efim Sandler)

A sequence of stills from a video showing a Russian Su-25 dropping a bomb on Chechen targets in early December 1994. The bomb eventually missed militant positions and hit a civilian neighborhood killing several people. (Efim Sandler collection).

The ground based air defences of the airbases around Chechnya included elements of 933 Separate Rocket Air Defence Regiment operating 9K332 Tor-M2 (NATO SA-15 Gauntlet) or possibly 9K37 Buk-M1 (NATO SA-11 Gadfly), and of 418th Rocket Air Defence Regiment, operating 9K33M2 Osa-AK (NATO SA-8 Gecko). The ground units also employed their integral Air Defence components with 9K35 Strela-10 (NATO SA-13 Gopher), ZSU-23-4 Shilka, 2K22 Tunguska, and 9K38 Igla MANPAD (NATO SA-18 Grouse).

Since the end of November, Russian Su-24MR jets were conducting reconnaissance missions over Chechnya. By 29 November, there were about 140 attack jets (Su-25 and Su-24) deployed at several airfields of North-Caucasian Military District. At the same time, 55 helicopters (Mi-24, Mi-8 and Mi-6) of Army Aviation were deployed at the airbases of Kizlyar, Beslan and Mozdok. About 30 airplanes of Transport Aviation started the transfer of military personnel and equipment to Mozdok and Beslan. 12 Mi-8MT of Internal Troops were also deployed.

On 1 December, Russian aviation performed its most famous action of the war – attacking the concentrations of Chechen aviation at Kalinovskaya and Khankala, in the morning and later, during the day – Grozny-Severny airport. The airstrikes continued through the night with the air full of illuminating munitions deployed by long-range aviation bombers. In total, Russians performed 198 sorties including 71 attack missions by Su-25 and Su-24, reportedly destroying 177 aircraft and four aviation ammunition depots.

The majority of the weapons deployed were unguided rockets and small calibre bombs (FAB-100 and FAB-250), as Russian pilots had the order not to damage the runways. The raid met with very light return fire from AAAs and small arms, while the Chechens reported only one man lost when a bomb or rocket hit the ZU-23-2 position. Despite impressive numbers, this action can be considered as a pure 'show-of-force' as there was no practical sense to destroy all the aircraft – Chechen aviation, even in theory, could not oppose incoming Russian troops. Needless to say, no Chechen aircraft ever attempted to take off.

Starting on the same day, 1 December, Russian attack jets were engaging targets elsewhere in Chechnya. Interestingly, no major infrastructure objective was hit but the majority of airstrikes were performed by lone aircraft towards the Chechen positions on the outskirts of Grozny. This eventually, caused little damage to entrenched Chechen fighters but resulted in numerous civilian casualties.

Engineers

Most of the units that came to the area of operations were lacking dedicated engineering units thus, it was decided to assign the profile units of Engineering Corps and therefore build the Engineering Corps Group in the area of operations. The core of the Engineering Force Group was based on two battalions – one of 170th Engineering-Sapper Brigade and one of 173rd Pontoon-Bridge Brigade, of the North-Caucasian Military District. The major task was to assemble the passage over Terek River, while secondary tasks were to provide engineering support for incoming forces, integrating the elements of 170th Brigade into OODs (Traffic Support Detachments).

Unfortunately, some of the units like the battalion of Moscow Military District based, 1st Engineer-Sapper Brigade, arriving in Mozdok on 8 December 1994, proved to be totally unprepared and had to be taken to reserve and conduct extensive training of the personnel.

The Group of Engineering Corps assembly mostly passed without glitches (except the 1st Independent Engineering Regiment). The mobile element of the joint battalion of 170th ESBr, including 42 men and 14 vehicles, marched from Kavkazskaya to Mozdok covering about 450km, whilst the rest of the battalion and heavy armour, were transported by railways – 56 men, six UR-77 and an IMR-1. Needless to say, the situation in the Engineering Corps was not different from other Russian military units – the battalions were actually the size of companies.

The joint battalion of 173rd Brigade was no exception – in order to take the PMP pontoons from the storage depot, the unit had to be reinforced by the drivers from 92nd Engineering Base (m/u 29235) based in Georgievsk. The battalion included 137 personnel and 40 vehicles and after a 105km march, camped near Mozdok. The battalion of 1st Brigade from Moscow District made a 215km march from Rostov-Yaroslavsky to Chkalovsky airbase but due to poor organisation it was late by about 5 hours. It was transferred to Mozdok by four flights in An-124 Ruslan cargo planes.

On 8 December, the assembly of Engineering Corps Group was finalised and included:

- Mozdok direction – Battalion of 170th Engineering-Sapper Brigade, Battalion of 173rd Pontoon-Bridge Brigade, Company of 131st Motor-Rifle Brigade, Battalion of 106th Airborne Division, Platoon of 56th Airborne Brigade, Squad of 92nd Engineering Base.
- Beslan and Vladikavkaz directions – Separate Battalion of 19th MRD, Company of 693rd MRR, Battalion of 76th Airborne Division, Platoon of 45th Special Forces Regiment, Platoon of 21st Airborne Brigade.
- Kizlyar direction – Battalion of 20nd MRD, Company of 255th MRR.
- Reserve – Battalion of 1st Engineering-Sapper Brigade.

To support the troops moving over six routes, each Route had a dedicated Engineering Detachment of Traffic Support (OOD) that was tasked with breaching obstacles both natural and man-made, demining of routes, bridges and pipelines, creating bypass routes and traversable passages over the rivers and water flows using bridge-laying equipment like MTU-72 and TMM. Each OOD of Internal Troops included IMR-2, excavator, crane, three BTR-80, mobile generators, three sets of UR-83P and KShM R-145BM. In addition, there was a special detachment in reserve of Engineering Corps of the North-Caucasian Military District that included KMT-7 equipped tank, IMR, UR-77, MTU-20 and BTR-80s.

An interesting image of Russian Electronic Warfare setup near Vladikavkaz pictured on 7 December 1994. Note the R-381 Taran complex (round antenna). (Efim Sandler collection)

The Group of Engineering Corps was increased by the units constantly arriving into the combat zone and by Jan–Feb 1995, included nine battalions, 19 companies and seven platoons with 1,198 men and 116 vehicles. In addition, the reserve of the Group has been increased to six battalions with 933 men and 57 vehicles, each from 210th Brigade, 57th Brigade, 110th Brigade, 71st Brigade, 315th Brigade and 316th Brigade.

Signalling and Electronic Warfare (EW)
The units of EW were deployed to Chechnya from 11 August 1994, mostly to monitor and report on the activity of Dudaev's forces, as part of the Russian effort to support opposition forces. The first results were reported in October–November when the first fixed network of Dudaev's forces has been mapped, operating between Mozdok and Grozny on the frequency of 127 MHz. By the start of the Russian operation in Chechnya, the major tasks of the EW units deployed to Chechnya were as following:

- Reconnaissance of radio networks and radio directions of Chechen units
- Radio-electronic suppression of systems and assets of military management, radio and TV channels of Chechen government
- Radio-electronic counter-measures to Chechen EW and radio-intelligence activities
- Providing electromagnetic compatibility of the EW in the units to ensure smooth performance environment

The initial Group of EW included 1919th Separate Battalion of R-EW-N (Radio-Electronic Warfare and Navigation – m/u 60039) and 1077th Separate Battalion of EW based in Mozdok, and EW unit of XLII Army Corps in Vladikavkaz. In addition to the nominal assets, 1919th Battalion deployed six outposts of radio-intelligence covering Short Waves and Ultra-Short Waves communications. A flight of Mi-8 helicopters (two Mi-8PPA and one Mi-8MTPP) was put on 30 min alert in the airfields of Mozdok and Budennovsk. The technical assets of the Group EW included:

- R-330B/T – 3 units
- R-378A/B – 3 units
- R-934U
- R-235U
- R-381T1
- R-381T2

In the later stages, the dedicated EW units were established in VIII and LXVII Corps, as well as in 131st, 135th and 136th Brigades, including two to three jamming stations R-330A/B, one to two jamming stations R-378 (R-325), one jamming station of aviation communications R-934U and various communication means.

Despite all the technological superiority there were issues that took some time to overcome. The first was the poor synchronisation with Joint Group units and the fact that many Russian commanders had little, if any, understanding how to use the EW. It was causing absurd situations when working for one unit, the EW was jamming frequencies of another unit.

The second, was extensive usage of civilian portable radios of Johnson, Alinco and Motorola models – that were never a target for Russian EW – being focused on military communication systems. It took some time and was not until those models were studied by Russian engineers, that effective measures were applied.

The last and probably the most interesting issue was that of translation. By the beginning of hostilities, all Chechen communications were performed in Chechen language that Russian operators were not familiar with. It took a while until the Russians started to hire reliable Chechen-speaking personnel, mostly via FSB/FSB, to work in the surveillance units.

The signalling means of the Joint Group deployment at first were provided by the Ministry of Transportation, Civil Aviation, Military District and State Communications. The communications hubs were established similar to those in Mozdok, equipped with cable stations P-296 and P-274, and wireless R-409 and R-415. They were connected to the cable network that was previously established by 182 Guards TBAP based in Mozdok until November 1994.

The first mobile communication hub was based upon the 136th Separate Motor-Rifle Brigade of XLII Army Corps, to communicate between Mozdok and Kizlyar with VIII Army Corps. The hub was based on R-440, N-18, R-161A2M and channels of space communications connected to R-409 station. At the start of the operation, the communication network included two mobile hubs of space communications, based on three fixed hubs and 14 stations of space links. In the direction of Tolstoi-Yurt, a major communication hub No. 301, was established (call-sign Gradus, Rus-Degree) by the means of 446th Separate Radio-Relay Cable Battalion (m/u 67275) with two R-412A and three R-409 stations.

With advance to Grozny, the major communication hub of Russian forces was established on Mount Yastrebinaya, about 8km from Grozny, serving North and East Groups. The hub operated the following equipment:

- R-410M – three pieces
- R-415 – five pieces
- P-257-24V
- P-246
- R-409 – eight pieces
- R-419 – two pieces
- R-414 – two pieces
- R-142N – five pieces
- P-244TN
- D-12
- D-13 – two pieces.

The hub provided 99 channels of secured communications, in the southern direction, hub No. 303 was established connecting Beslan and Vladikavkaz units. The work was done by 395th Separate Radio-Relay Cable Battalion (m/u 22520) and 551st Separate Signalling Battalion (m/u?) of XLII Army Corps. Very soon it became obvious that the signalling support for the operation was inadequate due to several reasons – obsolete equipment, insufficient number of trained personnel and inadequate organisational structure of combat units that had no dedicated signalling sub-units, to name a few.

Available signals units were sufficient only to support communications between the General Staff, divisions and regiments. It became obvious that there were no good means of communications at battalion level, some companies and platoons did not have dedicated communication means or assigned frequencies. The lack of communication obviously proved difficult for example, when companies had to communicate using regimental frequencies leading to a chaos in the air.

As for hardware, the Russian military did not pay much attention to supply troops with modern technology – from an overall amount of portable radios, only 10 percent were of the latest models. The majority of battalion radios were old and cumbersome R-123, R-159, R-158 and R-148, but even those were subject to technical malfunctions and a lack of batteries. Moreover, most of the signalling companies had no charging stations. It appears that the new devices of R-163 and R-165 models were never supplied to the combat units.

The General HQ took the task of conquering Chechnya very enthusiastically, possibly too much – there was a type of euphoria and it looked like old fellows were playing a board game. Interestingly, Russian General HQ never considered any other opposition hotspots than Grozny in a common belief that losing key republic infrastructure would bring Chechen leadership to surrender.

The real-time intelligence was non-existing – at least at the high levels of planning. According to numerous accounts, no-one ever considered a real war but a kind of 'show-of-force' move that had worked previously in Azerbaijan, Armenia, Georgia and even Moldova. This can be seen while looking through the Order of Battle – half of the forces are those of the Ministry of Interior and not the real combat troops capable of fighting a conventional war. No-one ever considered the real resistance to the 'mighty Russian Army'.

In his interview, General Lev Rokhlin, said:

The plan developed by General HQ became factually the plan for the troop death. It was not justified by any kind of operational-tactical consideration and did not take in account all the factors and settings. In fact, this plan was an adventuristic affair that led to the death of hundreds of soldiers.

Anticipating the worst, Dzhokhar Dudaev tried to reach to Boris Yeltsin, calling Moscow numerous times but with no success. The President of Ingushetia, the Afghan War hero, Ruslan Aushev, tried to assist but with the same results. Reportedly, Yeltsin was informed about Dudaev's efforts (at least via the Head of President Security Service, Aleksander Korzhakov) but remained irresponsive taking the position, 'we do not talk to bandits'.

On 6 December, the Minister of Defence, Pavel Grachev, and the Minister of Interior, Victor Yerin, met with Chechen leaders in Sleptzopskaya (Ordzhanikidzhe) Village, at the border between Chechnya and Ingushetia. Dudaev was accompanied by Z. Yandanbiev, M. Udugov, S. Basaev and B. Gelaev. By the end of the day, Grachev and Dudaev had a private conversation that, according to Grachev's memory, looked like the following:[2]

'Dzhokhar, it's your last chance and let's talk as military professionals. Can we resolve it peacefully with no blood unlike Afghanistan? Do you think you can fight against us? I will break you down in any case.'

'Are you seriously meaning the war?'

'Indeed. The decision has been made. But there is still a chance to back off.'

'I cannot back off, there are many others who will make it happen.'

'Thus, it will be a war'

'Let's be a war.'

'Dzhokhar, I will smash you like the God would do to a turtle.'

'Everything in Allah's hands!'

On the same day, General Mityukhin conducted a summary brief that was open to reporters. He discussed the blockade of Grozny and emphasised the usage of artillery and aviation to suppress any Chechen strongholds that would emerge on the way. This show was targeted to scare Chechens who, in turn, were not impressed at all. On 9 December 1994, President Yeltsin issued Decree No. 2166 backed up by a Russian government Decree No. 1360 ordering the North-Caucasian Military District to perform a special operation to block and disarm Chechen rebel forces. As a result, Decree No. 2166 can be seen as declaration of war as it overrode the previous one (No. 2137c) that gave the situation a chance for a peaceful resolution. On the same day, the Ministry of Defence issued Directive No. 312/1/006sh, ordering forces to move in from three directions towards Grozny and force Chechen militants to give up their weapons, otherwise take over the city. The war had been launched.

10
MOVING TO WAR

Between 05:00 and 08:00 on the morning of 11 December 1994, Russian forces entered Chechnya from three major directions, along six different routes.

Mozdok Group, commanded by General Chilindin, used Routes 1 and 2 and with 131st Separate Motor-Rifle Brigade, led the advance over Route 1 towards Pervomaiskaya, followed by the 81st and 451st PONs who were placed on outposts to protect roads and perform checking procedures for locals. 131st Brigade moved about 80km with no opposition and by 15:00, gathered some 2km east of Ken-Yurt without losses, while 81st PON took over the high ground near Petropavlovskaya and 451st PON near Podgornoe.

Interestingly in Ken-Yurt, Russian forces spotted two T-62 tanks, two T-72 tanks and a couple of BTR-60 APCs belonging to opposition forces. It was decided to destroy the T-62 tanks and BTRs but take T-72 and use them as towers – both tanks had main gun damages. The forces moving over Route 2, commanded by General Sigutkin, Deputy Commander of Airborne Corps for combat training, included the joint regiment of 106th Airborne Division and joint battalion of 56th Separate Airborne Brigade, followed by elements of the Internal Troops.

The units made it over Tersk Ridge with some delays related to heavy vehicles that had difficulties managing the elevation and icy conditions, but by 18:00, all elements gathered some 5km south-west of Komarovo. Both convoys moved over the area mostly controlled by opposition forces of Umar Avturkhanov, therefore the locals mostly welcomed them without any hostile actions. The only issues encountered were bogged armour and commanders losing orientation and moving in the wrong directions. Sergey Shestopalov of 137th Guards Airborne Regiment, 106th Tula Guards Airborne Division describes the order of movement of the Airborne Corps units:

> The Airborne Corps elements included joint battalion of 51st Guards Airborne Regiment commanded by Regiment Deputy Commander, Lieutenant-Colonel Vladimir Krymsky, joint battalion of 137th Guards Airborne Regiment commanded by Vladimir Alekseenko, SPA Battalion of 1182nd Guards Artillery Regiment commanded by Major Vladimir Kulikov, and a group of 56th Separate Airborne Brigade … Our airborne battalion moved under command of Chief HQ Officer of 106th Tula Division, Colonel Stanistav Semenyuta, while the Chief Operational Officer was Mikhail Zdanenya. Left behind was an airfield constantly receiving IL cargo planes with men and weapons.

> The convoy has been assembled in the mixed mode of wheeled and tracked vehicles that later proved itself. The leading was the tank with the mine-roller, followed by recon company of Senior Lieutenant Mikhail Teplinsky, call-sign 'Vyuga' (Rus – Blizzard), with the OOD – Traffic Support Detachment sappers. Following was 9th Airborne Company of Captain Alexander Borisevitch, call-sign 'Rybak' (Rus – Fisherman), then the major forces – self-propelled battalion of 1182nd Regiment, call-sign 'Baikal', 8th Airborne Company of Senior Lieutenant Konstantin Sokolenko, Battalion HQ and Sapper Company of Captain Anatoly Tupotin. The closing was 7th Airborne Company commanded by Captain German Makarov with the battalion support and supply vehicles.

Vladikavkaz Group, commanded by General Chindarov, used Routes 3 and 4. At 07:00, the elements of 76th Airborne Division and 21st Separate Airborne Brigade moved from their camping area in Chermen, Ingushetia, towards Verkhnie Achaluki, followed by 47th PON of Internal Troops. Reaching Verkhnie Achaluki at 11:00, the convoy was blocked by a crowd of locals with women, elders and children at the front, followed by men armed with hooks and spears trying to damage the vehicles. Russians, banned from using force against local population, tried to negotiate and even fired several shots in the air, but with no success. Seven vehicles were damaged and four set on fire and completely destroyed – the convoy turned

Chechen ZU-23-2 in Grozny's central square near the President's Palace, pictured on 7 December 1994. (Photo by Michael Evstafiev)

away from the village and camped in the field. At this point, it was decided to bring the convoy back and switch to the Mozdok direction after resupplying the troops.

At the same time, a company of 21st Brigade operated on a specially equipped train. The force commanded by an Airborne Battalion Commander, Major Sergey Stvolov, used what was called 'armoured train' though not really armoured – there were a locomotive, two passenger cars and several open platforms protected by 22,500 sandbags instead of armour, the weapons included three ZU-23-2 AAA, 82mm 2B9 Vasilyok mortar battery and a battery of SPG-9 recoilless rifles plus an R-142N communication vehicle. Ironically there was no particular assignment for such a train and its team, as nobody in Group HQ had ever heard of it.

Major Stvolov received very general orders to move in towards Grozny and give cover for the advancing troops. The train moved to Nazran and further into Chechnya but could not contact any of the troops until it reached Sleptsovskaya, where Dudaev militants blew up the railway bridge just in front of the paratroopers. Fortunately for the Russians, the train managed to stop and there were no casualties, however, it had to turn back towards Nazran. Upon reaching Nazran, it appeared that the locals had dismantled about 25 metres of tracks and the train stuck. During the night, paratroopers, with the help of three train operators and two officers from the Railway Corps, managed manually to recover the tracks and kept moving to reach Beslan by next morning. By then, the idea of using an 'armoured train' vanished and the company was directed to Route 4.

On Route 4, the advance was led by 693rd MRR followed by 46th PON of Internal Troops. The movement of the troops met with fierce opposition from the locals. On the approach to Nazran, a crowd of about 2,000 men, which also included armed local militia, attacked the leading units and managed to destroy about 16 vehicles. Three BTRs and four vehicles were damaged near Barsuki village. Near Yardynka, 15 vehicles were burnt including a T-72B1 tank.

At 17:45 the convoy was attacked by small arms fire near Gazi-Yurt, which led to the first casualty of the war – Private Vitaly Maslennikov of 693rd MRR was killed. Leaving about 70 vehicles behind, the convoy had to retreat to its initial positions. Later, in the same place, the convoy of Group medical unit was attacked by locals, wounding three medics, one of them later died from the injuries. On the morning of 12 December, the Commander of the Joint Group of Forces, General Mityukhin, called the newly appointed Commander of XLII Army Corps, General Troshev and in a very arrogant manner, ordered him to check the situation – why has the convoy got stuck in Nazran?

Troshev sent Colonel Eduard Vitsenets, Chief Education Officer of the Corps, who witnessed the absurdity of the situation as soldiers were not allowed to do anything and officers looked totally unprepared.

The things I've seen were unthinkable. Without any combat actions 40 vehicles were burnt down – about a third of the whole convoy. Two teenagers of 13–14 years old with spears instantly pinched all wheels of my jeep.

During the day, the Group lost 68 vehicles and had to pull back.

According to the plan, Kizlyar Group, commanded by General Lev Rokhlin, was supposed to move over Routes 5 and 6 from Dagestan. On the morning 11 December, the leading 57th PON of Internal Troops moved over Route 5 with the task of taking the road to Khasavyurt, under control. The 2nd Battalion, commanded by Lieutenant-Colonel Vitaly Seryogin, with 120 officers and soldiers, had the task of setting up the outposts along the road, moving from Baba-Yurt to the south.

Initially, the Russians did not expect any kind of opposition in the area but from the very beginning, it became obvious that the task was near to impossible. Locals behaved very aggressively with drivers provoking accidents with military vehicles causing them to

T-72A tanks of 693rd Motor-Rifle Regiment (Vladikavkaz Group) pictured on 11 December, prior to entering Chechnya. (Photo by TASS)

Major Oleg Dedegkaev (1st right), 57th Operation Regiment of Internal Troops deputy commander and head education officer. (via Efim Sandler)

later stop and become surrounded by crowds of locals. The locals also reacted by pushing forward a wave of screaming elders and women, to attract attention of the troops, while the men, armed with sticks and metal rods, came from behind, attacking the soldiers, hitting them and taking their weapons.

One of the trucks carrying the ammunition was stopped and about 50 men managed to unload its cargo and take it to the nearby village. The situation was saved by the Reconnaissance Company of 57th PON, led by the Chief of Regiment Reconnaissance, Major Vyacheslav Afonin. The BMPs running all over the place, managed to scare the crowd and release the vehicles.

Approaching Khasavyurt, the convoy became surrounded by a large number of locals backed up by dozens of fully armed men. This time, the soldiers were threatened with death unless they surrendered. Several vehicles managed to turn back but four BTRs and one truck were blocked and their crews taken hostages – soldiers still did not dare to open fire at the locals and mostly stayed inside the vehicles. 46 men of 2nd Battalion including its commander, Lieutenant-Colonel Seryogin and Chief of 57th PON Reconnaissance, Major Afonin, were taken and locked in one a Khasavyurt school basement.

At the same time, one of the BTRs with 11 crew that escaped from captivity, tried to get back to friendly forces but became lost and after 8 hours of driving through unfamiliar terrain, found themselves in the middle of an unknown village in Chechnya where they were captured. During the day, 57th PON commanders performed several attempts to negotiate the release of hostages whilst Deputy Commander and Chief Education Officer of the Regiment, Major Oleg Dedegkaev, twice, personally went to Khasavyurt to meet with local authorities. By the end of the day, he was also taken hostage during his third visit.

In total, there were 58 men of 57th PON captured in Khasavyurt (47) and 11 of the BTR crew taken in Chechnya. On the night of 11–12 December, a group of eight hostages, mostly officers, were transported to Grozny. On the next day, Deputy Commander of Internal Troops, Lieutenant-General Stanistav Kovun, flew to Khasavyurt and managed to release 39 hostages – probably all the remaining in Khasavyurt. Another 20 or 21 (probably including two men captured from other units), were kept in Grozny in the custody of Dudaev's Chief of Security, Abu Arsanukaev. Two more soldiers of 57th PON were released by the end of December and traded for captured Chechens, while 18 or 19 officers and soldiers remained prisoners as of 31 November 1994.

The major force of General Rokhlin's Group planned to use Route 6 but Rokhlin decided to change it as his scouts reported that the route was full of militants and preset ambushes – it appeared the plan had been compromised. Experienced 'Afghan Fox', Rokhlin ordered to work out a fake route and sent his men to 'coordinate' this route with locals – the route led the convoy from Kizlyar to Khankala via Khasavyurt, Gudermes and Argun. The real one was planned to move further north from Chechen border, bypass the major settlements towards Terekli-Mekteb then turn sharp back to Kumli and straight south, to take over Chervlennaya, to secure the pass over Terek River and bring Group forces to Tolstoi-Yurt.

The shift to Terekli-Mekteb over no-man's land was originally proposed by Deputy Commander of Internal Troops of North-Caucasian Military District, General Mikhail Labunets, who planned to move with the leading 63rd PON and secure Chervlennaya. Approved by Colonel General Anatoly Kulikov, it was presented to Lev Rokhlin who considered it ambitious but not impossible, and finally accepted. Only several senior officers knew of the real plan. For example, the commanders of the Chechen opposition forces who waited for General Labunets and 63rd PON on the way from Khasavyurt, never spotted him nor his Regiment.

This was exactly what Rokhlin needed – the convoy of VIII Army Corps led by Internal Troops started to move from Kizlyar at 13:25 and disappeared. During the night, there was complete radio silence and even the use of flashlights was strictly prohibited. Dudaev's forces tried to fire illuminating rounds and even several salvos of BM-21 Grad rockets but hit nothing.

On the night of 11–12 December, 63rd PON took over Chervlennaya without any opposition and reached the northern bank of Terek River. The only losses were several vehicles that got mired in the fields and could not be pulled out. The same night, at the commanders brief, Lev Rokhlin, already informed about the misfortunes of 57th PON at Khasavyurt, took the unit (57th PON) to the other side – he ordered to respond decisively to any hostile action from the locals. His orders were very direct – he ordered to open fire with all available means, including tank and heavy artillery in the mode, 'take them down, kill them all'. At this point, for Lev Rokhlin and his Group, the games were over and the real war started. He ordered VIII Corps artillery to get closer to forward positions and cover every movement of his Group; the VIII Corps were the one of the best trained troops in the Joint Forces Group.

The first day of the operation was over – only the Mozdok Group of General Chilindin managed to accomplish all the objectives and suffered no losses. Two other groups met tough opposition and sabotage and did not even reach Chechnya. Close to 100 vehicles were lost, one soldier killed and 58 taken hostages. Dozens were wounded. The first day explicitly showed that the Russian forces

Screenshot from dramatic footage taken in Nazran, Ingushetia, where the locals blocked the convoy of 693rd Regiment destroying at least 15 vehicles and forcing it to turn back. (Efim Sandler collection)

Russian soldiers captured on 11 December 1994 pictured during the meeting with journalists in the President's Palace in Grozny on 27 December. First from the left is 2nd Battalion Commander, Lieutenant Colonel Seryogin, third is Major Dedegkaev. Vitaly Seryogin was released on 19 August 1995, Oleg Dedegkaev was tortured and died from his wounds. (Photo by Misha Japaridze)

Frames showing Russian vehicles burning on the first day of operation – 11 December 1994. (Efim Sandler collection).

were not prepared and the war had not started yet – the troops acted as it was one of numerous pacifying operations of the late 1980s, early 1990s.

One could ask – was there such aggression from the side of Ingush and Dagestan population? The answer came on 4 December 1994 when Dzhokhar Dudaev initiated an emergency session of the Confederation of Caucasian People where he conveyed a message of incoming genocide of Caucasian people by Russians as happened during Stalin's times. Dudaev knew very well that the majority of the common population of Caucasian Republics, leaving those close to the borders of Chechnya, would not recall that he had squeezed Ingush and other non-Chechen people out of Chechnya just one to two years ago. However, the buzzword of Caucasian Genocide worked well.

Delegates from Dagestan, Chechnya, Ingushetia, North Ossetia, Kabardino-Balkaria, Karachay-Cherkessia, Adygea and Abkhazia were presented with a statement from the Commander of Confederation Armed Forces, Shamil Basaev, to perform actions against the incoming Russian troops – blocking the vehicles, sabotaging roads and communications, hitting Russian servicemen and members of their families.

Besides the practical sabotage of the Russian advance by the common people, Dudaev also received support from the leadership. For example, after the fierce opposition in Nazran, the President of Ingushetia, Ruslan Aushev, sent a request to the General Prosecutor Office of Russia, to perform a full investigation of Russian military actions against the civilian population that resulted in five killed, 15 wounded, six houses and one mosque destroyed.

Such information was never delivered to a wider Russian Federation audience but the Military Intelligence and FSB were well informed; the problem being that such information never reached decision makers or was deliberately neglected. For example, the Chief Intelligence Officer of North-Caucasian Military District, Major-General Vladimir Nesterov sent the following message:

> To Chief Military Intelligence Officers of Joint Group of Federal Forces
>
> By the means of Military District Intelligence, it was revealed that in the recent days there was a sharp increase of young Chechens from mountain regions arriving to the settlements of Naursk District – Lipatovo, Ischerskaya, Rubezhnoe, Znamenskoe. Over a half of them armed with weapons. In accordance with local authorities orders the hospitals are forcing the patients out to get prepared for accepting the wounded.
>
> A KamAZ truck loaded with small weapons arrived in Bratskoe settlement. Armour and ammunition are getting hidden under the piles of hay or straw placed in the private household premises.
>
> In Gvardeyskoe settlement, there is a detachment of Zavgaev supporters armed with small weapons, RPG and operating one BMP.
>
> In Ischerskaya settlement we revealed up to 80 Dudaev supporters armed with automatic weapons, RPG, three T-72 tanks, one BTR-70, three D-30 howitzers and two ZU-23-3 anti-aircraft artillery pieces.
>
> Mozdok, 10 December 1994
> General Nesterov.

During the day, army aviation flew dozens of sorties that were formally assigned to cover the advancing forces, but most probably, the actual task was reconnaissance and show-of-force. Despite official information that aviation never opened fire, Mi-24 gunships performed several attacks following the incoming fire from the ground. By the end of day, 11 December, the Russian Ministry of Defence reported that all missions have been accomplished and the forces reached all their objectives, blocking Grozny from three directions, without suffering any casualties. Clearly, this was far from the reality.

11
FIRST CLASHES

The first major engagement between advancing Russian and Chechen forces occurred on 12 December near the village of Dolinsky, some 25km north-west from Grozny, sitting on one of the major routes to the city. The village also hosted an oil storage facility. During the previous day, the commander of Chechen local defence unit, Vakha Arsanov, received a report from one of his men of incoming Russian units, he immediately contacted Aslan Maskhadov and requested to give him BM-21 Grad launchers. During the night, Arsanov's men prepared positions on one of the hills near Dolinsky overseeing the road (R-307).

In the afternoon of 12 December, upon reaching the vicinity of Dolinsky, the advancing convoy of 106th Airborne Division consisted of two joint battalions of 137th and 51st Regiments followed by 1182nd Artillery and 56th Brigade. From a distance of about eight kilometres, the scouts reported the presence of Chechen vehicles and directed two Mi-24 gunships to confirm observations. The pilots made several passes and confirmed the enemy position facing the road with two BM-21 launchers, two tanks and two BTRs. The report went to the commander of the convoy that was closing in on Dolinsky but could not make visual contact due to the hilly landscape.

Mi-24 reports went to the convoy's commanding group with Chief Intelligence Officer of Airborne Corps, Colonel Pavel Popovskih,

BMD-1 of Russian Airborne Corps pictured on 12 December 1994. Note the logs on the side of the vehicles. (Photo by Alexander Zemlianichenko)

and at the same time, to the aviation command HQ, General Ivannikov, requesting permission to attack. General Ivannikov instantly reported to the Joint Forces Commander, General Milyukhin, but the latter rejected permission as he feared it could cause damage to the oil facility and the pipe. After around 20 minutes, the gunships left the area and went back to base due to fuel shortages.

At around 14:00, Chechen Grads fired the first salvo at the elements of 51st Regiment and the following vehicles of 1182nd Regiment and the anti-aircraft battery of 56th Brigade, that were moving over the flat open terrain. The rockets found their targets. One of the 56th Brigade NCOs managed to spot the position of the coordinator of the Grads and reported it to his commander. Lieutenant-Colonel Vartsaba climbed the nearest hill bringing the D-30 and SPG team and requested to open fire from Group HQ. After his request was rejected, he nevertheless opened fire in the direction of the oil facility and hit one of the tall pipes that (presumably) had the Chechen spotter. After two hits, the pipe collapsed.

On the other side of the hill was a battalion of 137th Regiment and its commander, Lieutenant-Colonel Svyatoslav Golubyatnikov, instantly ordered his units to spread out and take positions under the cover of woods and hills. This was a timely move as the next Grad salvo landed directly on the spot where the vehicles of 7th Airborne Company were located. The Commander of 1182nd Artillery Battalion, Major Kulikov deployed 2S9 Nona battery, commanded by Captain Alexander Silin, who positioned the vehicles 150m apart in the middle of the battalion defences. The Reostat 1V119 of Kulikov, together with BMD-1KSh of Golubyatnikov and another BTR-D with paratroopers, climbed one of the hills to direct the Nona battery. About 10 minutes after the first rounds of Grad fire artillery, several hits were observed causing secondary explosions – probably hitting one of the vehicles or ammunition. After another 20 minutes, a pair of Mi-24 gunships arrived at the area but could not spot anything and having no permission to fire inside the village or to hit the oil storage facility, the gunships circled above the woods and even released several salvos of FFARs but with no obvious results.

Meanwhile the convoy of the 51st Regiment turned back and led by a T-72A tank with KMT-7 mine-roller, approached the positions of 56th Brigade anti-aircraft battery ready for attack. As usual, there was little coordination between the units and 56th Brigade men were ready to open fire taking the incoming force to be Chechens. Just moments before it was too late, one of 56th Brigade gunners shouted that they were 'friendlies' – he reasonably thought that Chechen tanks would not be equipped with mine-rollers riding over their own territory. In this instance, his sharp eye, and his flash thought about the KMT-7, saved lives. Apart from this, the rest was bad news.

The devastating results of the Chechen BM-21 Grad attack on the convoy of 106th Airborne Division near Dolinsky settlement on 12 December 1994. Note the BTR-DZ with ZU-23-2 mount. (Photo by TASS)

The first salvo hit 51st Regiment command BMD-1KSh and destroyed it, killing two senior officers – Colonel Evgeny Alexeeenko and Colonel Evgeny Frolov. In total, six men were killed and another one died in the hospital, 13 wounded. Two BMD, two Ural trucks and one GAZ-66 with ZU-23-2 were destroyed and another BMD was badly damaged. Chechen losses were never reported. The blame was put on the Joint Forces Commander General Mityukhin, who panicked and was afraid of making decisions. As a direct consequence, on 15 December he was relieved from duties by Minister of Defence, Pavel Grachev.

During the night of 12–13 December, the Chechens shelled the 106th Division's position near Dolinsky with Grad, tanks and artillery. This time, the paratroopers were not taken unguarded and did not suffer casualties. The units of 106th Airborne Division stayed near Dolinsky until 18 December 1994.

On the same day, 131st Brigade was tasked to move towards Pervomayskaya, over the Terk Ridge and secure the high ground over the settlement. The joint detachment of Brigade passed the Ridge without opposition but moving down towards Pervomayskaya, the leading vehicles of 3rd Motor-Rifle Company (CO Rustem Klupov) including a T-72A tank No. 524 (TC Lieutenant Evgeny Filonenko) came under small arms and artillery fire. The tank was hit and disabled while the crew managed to evacuate with only one lightly wounded.

According to Russian reports, the Chechens used a T-55 tank firing from inside the houses that were actually caponiers – this is most likely a mistake and the actual piece was a 100mm MT-12 Rapira anti-tank gun that was used to fire from barns, as in numerous other cases. The tank platoon of 3rd Tank Company started to fire from long-range, guided by infantry until it managed to hit several Chechen positions and silence the gun. The fire exchange lasted for about 3 hours then died down. At this point, the Russian advance stopped, the leading element took the defensive line towards Pervomayskaya and the main body of 131 Brigade assembled positions on the Terk Ridge.

On the other side, VIII Army Corps Detachment of General Rokhlin, reached Chervlennaya by the afternoon of 12 December. Commanders were met by the locals and requested not to enter the settlement but continue to the bridge over the Terek River.

Rokhlin and his officers respected the request and camped about 4km north, telling everybody that they would cross over the bridge the next morning. What happened later was totally in Rokhlin's style. With the oncoming darkness, he ordered 68th ORB (Separate Reconnaissance Battalion) to move towards Terek River and secure the bridgehead on the north side, while 63rd PON would bypass Chervlennaya and block it from the south so there would not be any surprises coming from Chechnya. On the same night, Chechen militants supported by armour, crossed the river over the bridge to attack the positions of VIII Corps but ran into the blocking 63rd PON. Despite coordination glitches, Rokhlin's artillery officers managed to direct artillery fire without any observers, considering that the Internal Troops were never trained to operate artillery.

During the following night, Engineers were tasked with breaching the safe pass for the armour through the railway tracks towards Terek River. After the members of 68th Battalion crossed the river and secured the bridgehead on the southern bank, 1st Bridge-Laying Battalion of 173rd Brigade, started to assemble the pontoon-bridge. The operation proved to be unique.

In accordance with the decision of the Chief Engineering Officer, the pontoon-bridge over the Terek River for the transfer of VIII Army Corps would be based on the PMP hardware and assembled by elements of 173rd Pontoon-Bridge Brigade of North-Caucasian Military District (homebase in Kamentsk-Shakhtinsky). The complex and changeable nature of the riverbed, the presence of islands and deep gullies washed in by the current and the high speed of the current, required the adoption of non-standard solutions and the equipment of a combined bridge, the middle part of which, about 50m long, passed along the washed-out sandy island. According to all existing canons, it is impossible to equip a bridge crossing under such conditions. However, the conditions of the situation required the construction of a crossing in this area, where the crossing of the 20th MRD was unexpected for the enemy and made it possible to reach the northern outskirts of Grozny along the shortest path with minimal losses.

Due to the conditions of the riverbed, each pontoon link was manually moved into the bridge alignment. With no means of mechanisation, boats, et cetera, it was impossible to apply. The pontoon builders worked in icy water and in heavy rain for a day, constantly being fired upon by the enemy from the opposite bank. With the advance detachment of the 20th MRD reaching the river, the aiming area was covered by motorised rifles and artillery. By 13:00 on 14 December 1994, the bridge was ready. At 14:00, 20th MRD elements began crossing the Terek River, making their appearance on the right bank suddenly for the enemy which did not allow for organised resistance.

The maintenance of the bridge was carried out in difficult conditions. The high opposite bank of the river demanded the arrangement of a congress. To strengthen it, entrance ramps of the PMP sections, reinforced concrete slabs, logs, et cetera, were used. Moreover, due to the high speed of the current (1.5–2.0m/sec), the coast was quickly eroded and after every 2–3 hours of crossing, the entrance was re-equipped and the bridge was lengthened by one river link. Part of the bridge, passing through the sandy island, required the construction of gates and constant strengthening with logs, gauge shields, lining from the PMP kit and other improvised materials.

To assist the 173rd Brigade engineers in the maintenance of the bridge, the Chief Engineering Officer transferred 50 men of 1st Engineering Brigade or Moscow Military District, kept in the Joint Group of Forces Reserve. The unit reached the bridgehead by 12:00 on 14 December bringing chainsaws and entrenching tools. The terrain conditions required a change in the traditional rectilinear shape of the bridge, which led to a slight decrease in the speed of vehicles, especially when cornering.

In total, over 480 vehicles of VIII Army Corps were transported over the bridge during the day.

In the Vladikavkaz direction, elements of joint regiment of 76th Guards Airborne Division, which included 165th Separate Reconnaissance Company (CO Senior Lieutenant Andrey Shevelev) and a battalion of 237th Guards Airborne Regiment (CO Lieutenant-Colonel Vyacheslav Sivko), ran into prepared Chechen positions located at the cattle farm of the Assinovskya settlement. Chechens tried to cut the leading group of Reconnaissance Company but Lieutenant Shevelev quickly organised a defensive line and ordered to open fire without proper authorisation, supported by fire from a battalion of 237th Regiment including ZU-23-2 and 2S9 Nona. Eventually, the permission to open fire was granted and also included airstrikes by jets that destroyed several buildings.

The troops managed to pass through and set positions in the open field between Assinovskaya and Novy Sharoy. Reportedly, there were losses on both sides including several civilians killed.

It is important to note that by then (until 17 December), the issue 'to open fire' was treated by Russian Command in a case-by-case manner and only as return fire. Even after the engagements of 13 December, Russians tried not to shoot until being hit. The numerous signs of armed militants did not trigger any reaction besides the attempt of senior officers to conduct negotiations. Very soon it would change.

On 14 December, Russian Aviation suffered its first loss – Mi-8T No.27 (Red 27) of 325th Separate Helicopter Regiment (m/u 62978) was hit by small arms and performed an emergency landing near Novy Sharoy. In the morning, the Vladikavkaz Group Army Aviation

The crew of Mi-8T No 27 (Red 27) of 325th Separate Helicopter Regiment that was hit by small arms and performed an emergency landing near Novy Sharoy. From left to right – Lieutenant Colonel Nikolai Leskov (commander), Captain Oleg Shaplygin (navigator), Senior Lieutenant Sergey Devyatkov onboard technical specialist. (Efim Sandler collection)

Logbook page of Yury Loktionov, Mi-24 Squadron Commander of 55th Separate Helicopter Regiment, showing three combat sorties flown on 11 December 1994, totalling four hours and 33 minutes. (Photo by Yury Loktionov)

based in Beslan, received a task of supporting leading units of 76th Airborne Division located near Assinovskaya. Acting Commander of Transport Helicopters Detachment, Lieutenant-Colonel Nikolai Leskov (Squadron Commander of 325th Regiment), took the assignment together with the crew of Captain Nikolai Malkov. The cover was provided by a pair of Mi-24Vs led by Lieutenant-Colonel Yuri Loktionov (Squadron Commander of 55th Separate Helicopter Regiment). Two Mi-8Ts were loaded with about 1.5 tons of provision.

Leskov mentioned that he and his navigator, Captain Oleg Shaplygin, were familiar with the landing zone but the visibility was very low – less than 1,000m thus, both elements should have been very close. The weather in Beslan was better – over 1,500m and over 150m of cloud edge. The group, led by Leskov, took the direction towards Nazran and then onto Novy Sharoy. Closing in on the landing zone, the visibility dropped significantly – less than 1,000m and less than 70m for cloud edge. Nikolai Leskov passed Assinovskaya and was requested by Mi-24V lead to check the direction – he responded that he knew what he was doing.

The Mi-24 pair leading thought that Leskov had been tasked with reconnaissance of the area as it was common practice to combine missions. Closing to Novy Sharoy, the Mi-24 lead once again requested to check the direction which took some time and the group almost reached Shaami-Yurt (some 15km from LZ). At this point, Lieutenant-Colonel Leskov probably realised the mistake and ordered a right turn. The visibility was even worse – the cloud edge almost 'touched the trees'. The group flew along the M-29 Federal Road (E50 highway) full of Chechen outposts.

Near the junction Samashki-Novy Sharoy, the pair of Mi-8s were attacked by grenade launchers and small arms from the nearby woods. The first grenade hit the leading Mi-8 and the second just missed the following one. Lieutenant-Colonel Leskov performed an emergency landing on the highway. Captain Malkov reported that his Mi-8 was hit and damaged. Lieutenant-Colonel Loktionov ordered Captain Malkov to return to base and another Mi-24 to escort him. Both helicopters flew back and Loktionov reported to General Ivannikov onboard the flying command post, An-26 from Mozdok, and received orders to remain in the area to wait for the Search and Rescue party. Meanwhile, he performed two runs along the road and tried to keep the Chechens off the downed helicopter, firing FFARs and machine gun, but also received very precise fire from several directions, including anti-aircraft artillery (probably ZU-23-2 installed on KamAZ trucks and DShK on the UAZ).

Approaching the area, the search and rescue Mi-8T escorted by a pair of Mi-24s, was also hit by small arms fire that killed one of the paratroopers of 21st Brigade onboard. Upon another version Mi-8 was on a routine reconnaissance flight and received a shift to another task by radio. After circling the area for about 30 minutes, all the time receiving small arms

Interesting image of Mi-8T red '27' taken on 16 December 1994 proving the Chechens tried to transport the helicopter to some place off the landing site. The helicopter was never found. (Photo by Georges DeKeerle)

fire, Lieutenant-Colonel Loktionov managed to return to Beslan and land on the last drops of fuel.

On the ground, the crew were surrounded by Chechens and after a short firefight, both Nikolai Leskov and Oleg Shaplygin were killed, whilst the technician, Senior Lieutenant Sergey Devyatkov was wounded in the legs and taken to the hospital in Achkhoy-Martan, where one leg was amputated. During the night he was transferred to Grozny and died from his wounds on 16 December 1994. The helicopter mysteriously disappeared and has been never found – possibly transported to one of the close farms and hidden in the barn.

With the return of Yuri Loktionov, Commander of Ground Forces Aviation, General Vitaly Pavlov, performed an investigation. The official reason named bad weather conditions which caused the loss of the orientation of Group Commander (Lieutenant-Colonel Leskov) which caused the group to overfly an area controlled by the enemy. Due to bad visibility and heavy group fire, Mi-24 was not able to assist Leskov's crew and had to return to Beslan after being hit.

Several things were not mentioned in the official version. It appeared that the maps of Mi-8 and Mi-24 helicopters were different. The Mi-24 gunship crews had the maps with all the forces marked and knew precisely where the friendlies and enemy positions were, which was updated constantly. For some reason, Mi-8 crew had 'clean' maps without such information. The reason being the Russian intelligence officers feared that such a map would become available to Chechens and reveal the location of Russian forces and information of Chechen positions. The absurdity of the situation was that the Chechens knew the location of Russian forces better than Russian intelligence officers.

Informally, many blamed Yuri Loktionov for being unhelpful, others blamed paratroopers or infantry of the Vladikavkaz Group in that they did not rush to the rescue. In both cases, the blames are unfounded as Lieutenant-Colonel Loktionov risked his crew and helicopter to stay in the area and returned to base with no fuel and 18 AAA hits. The ground units simply had no knowledge of what was happening in the air, as they had no access to Air Force channels. Even if they had the knowledge, the coordination and relevant approvals would have taken longer than the time available for the downed crew to hold against out the Chechens.

The intensity of the ground fire can be judged by the description of the damage to the Mi-8T flown by Captain Nikolai Malkov:

The alternating current switch box was smashed by a direct hit by a projectile, all the wires were torn out and hanging in the cargo compartment, there were multiple holes in the additional barrel, one of which a child could crawl through, the external fuel tanks were also pierced by an innumerable number, they could not get a single rocket from the UB-16 FFAR pods (all shot through), in the tail boom multiple hits of small bullets and shells of anti-aircraft guns, one of the shells exploded inside the beam in the area of the stabiliser, the fragments came out in a circle, breaking one of the control cables of the main rotor. On one of the engines, the gearbox was smashed by a direct hit by a projectile; upon arrival, not a single gauge worked on the helicopter, and much more …

This was the first loss of a Russian helicopter during the war but was not the first one lost to Chechen actions. On 29 July 1994, a Mi-8 helicopter (probably of Internal Troops) was destroyed on the ground in Miniralnye Vody airport during a failed operation to release hostages.

12
THE WAY TO GROZNY

Command Change and Reinforcements

From 15 to 20 December 1994, Russian forces mostly remained in position waiting for their orders. The main reason being that the Joint Forces Commander, General Mityukhin was called to Moscow and left the Group, connecting this with 'health issues'. It is interesting to note that during this period, when it became obvious that the operation would not be an easy trip, several Russian generals suddenly developed 'health issues'; for example, Commander of Mozdok Group, General Chilindin, had to be replaced with General Konstantin Pulikovsky.

On 17 December, Russian forces received probably one of the most faithful orders of the war – 'from 00:00 on December 18, 1994, all actions to disarm the illegal armed formations should be carried out in form of combat operations, with the integrated use of all means of destruction on objects, targets and firepower, including those located in populated areas'. At the same time, the Minister of Defence, Pavel Grachev, was constantly looking for the appropriate candidate to replace Mityukhin.

His first choice was the Deputy Commander of Ground Forces, General Eduard Vorobyov. Vorobyov refused on the basis that the troops were not ready and the operation had not been properly planned. Grachev exploded, blaming him in concealing the facts and not properly informing him personally, but Vorobyiv denied this, pointing that all information and reports were promptly submitted to the Ministry of Defence. Grachev threated him with a court-martial and demanded his instant resignation (later Eduard Vorobyov faced a lawsuit) – the 'show of the absurd' continued.

Unexpectedly, Lieutenant-General Anatoly Kvashnin, offered to head the Joint Group. Kvashnin was young and ambitious and at 48 had a fast career, whilst not being a professional officer, he decided to remain in the military and served mostly in HQ positions having no combat experience but excelling in all his appointments. Kvashnin received the rank of Major-General in 1984 (age 38), commanding 78th Tank Division based in Kazakhstan. During the last two years before the war with Chechnya, he acted as one of the commanding officers in the Chief Operational Directorate of Ministry of Defence, de facto planning the operation from October 1994.

Unlike General Mityukhin who looked old and tired, Anatoly Kvashnin looked young and energetic – although they were the same age. On 20 December, Pavel Grachev, by the Order No. 444, appointed Anatoly Kvashnin to command the Joint Group, while his Head of HQ became General Leonty Shevtsov. Kvashnin's position was very simple: 'I also graduated military academy and know how to manage the troops, besides there is nobody to fight

Russian BTR-80 in fresh colors pictured near Mozdok on 8 December 1994. (Photo by Misha Japaridze)

except several gangs of villagers.' The Commander of VIII Army Corps (Group North-East and later North), General Rokhlin who spent over 10 years in combat, was not very impressed considering Kvashnin another 'puppet'.[1] Shevtsov, on the other hand, enjoyed more respect within the troops, sometimes naming the Joint Group as the Shevtsov Group

The troops lodged over the wastelands of Chechnya with hardly any supplies. Meanwhile, more troops were called. Through several directives of General HQ, the Joint Group of Forces was reinforced starting from mid-December. On 14 December 1994, the joint battalion of 98th Guards Svirsk Airborne Division arrived in Mozdok. The Battalion was commanded by Lieutenant-Colonel Sergey Koblov, based on 3rd Airborne Battalion of 217th Airborne Regiment and included about 400 men in three companies – two on BMD-1 and one on GAZ-66, flame-throwing platoon (RPO-A), anti-aircraft platoon (three ZU-23-2 based on trucks), reconnaissance platoon and a battery of 2S9 Nona. Around the same time, the joint regiment of 104 Guards Airborne Division arrived in Beslan, including battalions of 337th and 328th Regiments. The VIII Army Corps 33rd MRR was deployed to Kizlyar. Upon the Directive of General HQ No. 312/1/00151 of 8 December 1994, the Ground Forces Command had to prepare and send to Chechnya four motor-rifle regiments – 81st MRR from Volga Military District, 129th MRR from Leningrad Military District, 276th MRR from Ural Military District and 503rd MRR from Moscow Military District.

The newly arriving units were of joint (or mixed) nature – being filled by assets from the various elements of the respective military districts. For example, the Ekaterinburg based 276th Regiment were a conserved unit with little manpower and almost no vehicles. The men were brought from the units of the District whilst the

Russian civilian Mi-26 helicopter unloading armour and troops of the Ministry of Interior in Mozdok, pictured on 16 December 1994. (Photo by AFP)

Convoy of Internal Troops of Kizlyar Group moving towards Tolstoy Yurt on 11 December. Note the PT-76 tanks of Mechanized Company of 8th Operational Brigade (8th BRON, m/u 3737). (Photo by Reuters)

Chechen S-60 anti-aircraft artillery pictured in December 1994. As with any other AAA system, it proved to be versatile working against airborne and ground targets, having a devastating effect on light armour. Due to limited mobility, most of the Chechen S-60s were either destroyed or captured by Russian forces during the first days of operation. (Efim Sandler collection)

vehicles were donated by neighbouring 324th and 105th Regiments. Interestingly, just before being sent to Chechnya, about 70 percent of officers and NCOs reported for discharge and thus, had to be replaced by volunteers and the 2-year committed officers from the other units. The situation with the Samara based 81st Guards Motor-Rifle Regiment, 90th Guards Tank Division, Volga Military District, was somewhat better in that it completed about 75–85 percent of the Peace-Time Schedule. The additions included a tank battalion (T-80B/BV) of 6th Guards Regiment, 90th Division and SPA Battalion of 589th Guards Motor Rifle Regiment, 27th Guards Motor-Rifle Division.

In total, 8st MRR had 1,414 soldiers and officers, 190 armoured vehicles (including 31 T-80, 81 BMP-2, 18 2S1) and 257 soft-skin vehicles. 129th Regiment was part of the Peace Keeping 45th Motor-Rifle Division and was trained to operate in a light anti-tank environment, having only BTR-70/80 APCs. The Regiment was reinforced by 133rd Separate Tank Battalion of T-80B/BV tanks.

Due to the urgent nature of the directives sent by General HQ to Military Districts, none of the units managed any kind of joint training and nor joint briefs – infantry did not know the tanks, tankmen did not know the infantry. In the chaos of rushing the units into the conflict area, many urgent and valuable assets were left behind, such as field kitchens and explosive plates for tank reactive armour (ERA).

On 20 December 1994, the Head of HQ of Operational Group of Ministry of Defence, General Leonty Shevtsov, sent a message to Head of HQ of Armed Forces about the alarming state of the incoming units:

Drawbacks have been revealed after checking the units for readiness to upcoming combat action. Those require additional time, efforts and assets to fix.

The lowest level has been shown by the regiment of Volga Military District. The main drawbacks:

◊ Officers, platoon and company commanders (about 50 percent), are not familiar with BMP-2
◊ Officers of mortar batteries of motor-rifle battalions are not ready to operate Vasilyok automatic mortars
◊ Officers of artillery battalion have very poor level of training (all 17 platoon leads are 'two-years' lieutenants from civilian colleges)
◊ Snipers, grenade launcher operators, machine gun operations never performed actual fire exercises with their respective weapons
◊ Signalling Platoon of 1st Motor-Rifle Battalion has no weapons or ammunition
◊ The elementary training to get personnel familiarised with weapons would take 7–10 days

The Fight for the Bridge

On 20 December, General Rokhlin, Kizlyar Group, after taking the positions near Tolstoi-Yurt, planned to move further towards Grozny over Sunzha River near the Petropavlovskaya settlement. According to scout reports, Chechens prepared the 60-ton bridge over Sunzha River for demolition while Petropavlovskaya hosted a large detachment. At 01:00, Rokhlin ordered 68th ORB (Major Dmitry Grebenichenko) to secure the bridge and probe the defences of Petropavlovskaya. Russians moved on the BTRs and at a safe distance, split into two parties – the main body of about 80 men moved towards the settlement while the small group of scouts under command of Senior Warrant Officer, Victor Ponomaryov, managed to reach the bridge and disarm the explosives without being spotted.

On the approach to Petropavlovskaya, the main group came under fire and became stuck on the ground. After 30 minutes, Russian soldiers – being low on ammunition – started to retreat under the cover of BTRs; many showed signs of confusion as it was their first combat. At this point, General Rokhlin, driving his UAZ vehicle, appeared on the battlefield and took the command over the fight. He walked from one position to another, guiding the soldiers showing them targets and kept standing high, expressing complete disregard for his own life. Later, Rokhlin recalled that this was his only chance of getting the soldiers to fight – by personal example.

The members of 68th ORB recovered and counter-attacked, managing to secure positions between Petropavlovakaya and the Sunzha River, supported by heavy tank and artillery fire.

In the morning, additional elements came to support the scouts of 68th ORB. The motor-rifle company of 81st PON was approaching the outskirts of Petropavlovskaya, when its commander, Senior Lieutenant Yuri Strukov, was mortally wounded by a sniper.

An immediate evacuation was called and the Mi-8MTV-2 helicopter of 5th Separate Mixed Air Squadron (m/u 3686) of Internal Troops was shot down while approaching the battlefield at 14:20. The helicopter was flying very low (20–30m) at the speed of 150km/h and came under small arms fire. After it was hit by RPG, it caught fire and crashed, killing the crew of Major Alexander Gasan and two officers of the medical team.

In the evening, the company of 81st PON moved into Petropavlovskaya but got lost and finally was ambushed on the open space near the administration building. The first destroyed was GAZ-66 with ZU-23-2; the fire nailed the Russians to the ground until a BTR managed to position itself between them and the Chechens but soon, it was destroyed by RPG. The BTR of commanding officer also received RPG and caught fire. The last BTR sped up and managed to leave the site safely.

The Order of Gallantry of Russian Federation No 0211 and report card, awarded to Squad Leader of 68th ORB, Konstantin Arabadzhiev, by the President's Decree of 6 January 1995, for his actions during the fight on the bridge over Terek River on 21 December 1994. This was one of the first Russian awards for the Chechen War. (Efim Sandler collection)

The forces of 81st PON, with support of tank, tried to recover the trapped men moving from two directions over the narrow streets, but was repelled by heavy fire. At this point, the Chechens realised they might be surrounded, especially with the fact that there were more and more Russian units approaching Petropavlovskaya – they started to back off and finally left the site, gathering on the outskirts.

In the early morning, 21 December, Chechens attacked positions of 68th ORB who were holding the bridge. The Russians were totally outnumbered and outgunned and so ordered a retreat of a small unit. The Group Commander and a soldier, Konstantin Arabadzhiev, remained to cover the retreat. The Group Commander Senior Warrant Officer, Victor Ponomaryov, was killed trying to evacuate a wounded soldier.[2] The Chechens, although taking over the bridge, could not secure it and prepared for demolishing it – the newly arrived elements of 104th Guards Airborne Division with the support of tanks, squeezed them out and took over. By 14:00, 68th ORB was replaced by a battalion of 337th Airborne Regiment of 104th Division and pulled back to Tolstoi-Yurt for recovery. One of the major roles in the fight for the bridge, was played by the tankmen of the 20th Separate Tank Battalion, commanded by Major Mansur Rafikov, and showing outstanding performance and skills.

During the two days of fighting, Lev Rokhlin Group lost 16 officers and soldiers in addition to five men from the downed helicopter. Dozens were wounded. 68th ORB and 81st PON had recover their losses. The number of Chechen casualties is not known but reportedly, there were dozens killed. However, the Group achieved its objectives and took positions some 8km from the outskirts of Grozny. On the night of 22–23 December, Chechens performed attacks on positions of a joint battalion of 238th Airborne Regiment, 104th Division, located near Vinogradnoe settlement. The intention to attack was revealed by the radio-intelligence units and timely reported to General Rokhlin Group HQ, which ordered to reinforce the positions of paratroopers with motor-rifle units and artillery.

The Fight of Alkhan-Kala

After spending several days near Assinovskaya, Vladikavkaz Group Command decided not to carry on over the E50 highway but to shift north, bypassing Samashki and move towards Grozny over the Tersk Ridge cutting towards Grozny between Oktyabr'skoe (north) and Alkhan-Kala (south). The reason is believed to be that a large number of Chechen opposition hotspots over the highway were revealed by aerial reconnaissance, which, due to the particular landscape, would cost too much in time and troops.

By 18 December, Head of HQ of Chechen Armed Forces, Aslan Maskhadov, ordered to set-up blocking positions at Alkhan-Kala and assigned the task to the newly formed, Galanchzhoy Regiment (GP), supported by numerous small groups from local villages. The GP Group of about 40 men, commanded by Shamsuddin Bunkhoev (a local of Samashki who ran a business in Volgograd) and who was one of the deputies of Regiment Commander, was reinforced by about the same number of locals arriving in two detachments. From 18 till 20 December, the Chechens prepared positions that included a concrete machine gun position remaining from the Second World War, a caponier for BTR, a position of D-30 howitzer and mortar and a number of trenches. In addition, a BM-21 was requested.

On the night of 20 December, two scout groups of Chechens reported an incoming Russian unit – leading 8th Airborne Company, 104th Airborne Regiment. Considering that the Russian vanguard was disconnected from the main body and consisted of about 1–2 companies, the plan was to split the force into four groups and wait until the Russians move down from the Ridge towards Alkhan-Kala, then fire the BM-21 into the main body and attack by GP, main force in the centre, two groups of locals on the flanks with one group in reserve. The plan was not coordinated with Maskhadov and was an amateur initiative that started to fail from the beginning. The BM-21 and D-30 opened fire that was totally imprecise – Grad rockets went off in an unidentified direction while several rounds of 122mm 3Sh2 Flechette, eventually reached the rear of the leading convoy but did not cause any damage as all the men were inside armour.

The paratroopers returned fire and disabled the D-30. Another version suggests that after two rounds, the breech lock got jammed and while trying to fix it, two of the crew were killed and one wounded. Later in the night, at about 02:00, the Group of GP moved towards the Russian positions and managed to get inside the perimeter as the Russian guards fell asleep. One of the paratroopers spotted them, yelled to alert his comrades, managed to reach a BMD-2 and started to fire instantly, killing several of attackers. The BMD was destroyed by RPG but the momentum was lost and the Chechens who found themselves in the middle of the battalion positions of 104th Regiment, were quickly gunned down. From 38 men, only 11 managed to get out, all of them wounded. Russian losses were one officer and two soldiers.

In the morning, the Russians were subjected to imprecise fire from the D-30 howitzer located at Oktyabr'skoe, ironically, one of the rounds hit 2S9 Nona's position of 237th Regiment, killing two of the crew. The same day, several Chechen commanders arrived at Alkhan-Kala, including Ruslan Gelaev, who confirmed the nonsense of attacking a missive Russian force by small groups and recommended a retreat towards Grozny. On 23 December, a Chechen BM-21 fired about 20 rounds towards 237th Regiment convoy with no success. On the next day, the battalion of 234th Regiment ran into the same type of ambush losing 2 (3) men and two BMDs.

Building the Force – Round 3

By the late December, when it became obvious that the number of troops was insufficient, the Ministry of Defence initiated another round, committing 74th MRBr, 166th MRBr, 324th MRR, 506th MRR and 245th MRR with all the units being planned to arrive in early January 1995. In addition to the Ground Forces, there were units of Airborne Corps and Naval Infantry that are discussed later. This round was even more absurd than the previous one. The regiments were not only conserved and had 10 times less personnel than required, but some of them had already donated their most capable officers, NCOs,

Chechen D-30 pictured at Pervomayskaya on 14 December 1994. Chechen artillery proved to be a huge 'splinter' for Russians – hard to spot and easy to operate, with deadly results. (Photo by Efim Sandler Collection)

soldiers and vehicles, to the regiments in the second round. Here is an example of Ekaterinburg based 324th Motor-Rifle Regiment (m/u 61931), 34th Motor-Rifle Division of Ural Military District:

- The motor-rifle battalions lacked majority of BMPs that were provided to 276th MRR in early December
- The whole tank battalion with all soldiers has been transferred to 276th MRR
- The artillery battalion minus anti-tank battery has been transferred to 276th MRR
- 70 percent of the officers and most of the NCOs were transferred to 276th MRR

What remained of 324th MRR was only a handful of officers and soldiers along with vehicles that were mostly junk as the better ones were supplied to 276th MRR just two weeks previously. In the anti-tank battery, there were only three men – commander and two platoon commanders who actually were '2-year' civil lieutenants with very limited experience. Interestingly, the battery was operated by BRDM-2 based 9P148 Konkurs ATGMs (NATO AT-5 Spandrel) since 1991 but no-one ever performed a single live-fire exercise, including its commander (the formal reason was a budget shortage to provide ATGMs for training).

At the end of December when the directive came to commit the Regiment to the combat zone, the majority of remaining officers and NCOs reported for discharge. Now it was the turn of 324th MRR to receive the remainder. It came from all units of the Ural Military District, including newly mobilised officers and NCOs from the reserve. The majority of the soldiers were either new with less than two months service (about 50 percent) or others, kicked out from their respective units due to various reasons. The Regiment had 10 days (22 December – 2 January) from the moment the directive was received, to the day it left for Chechnya over the railway.

Nevertheless, District Command reported that the Regiment was fully equipped and ready.

Regarding the units scrambled in late December and destined to be thrown into the grinder of the war in January, one of the Russian Generals wrote a report and summarised the failures.[3] The report eventually leaked to the press as did many documents of the period.

1. The personnel is not ready both mentally and physically for combat and actions in rough weather
2. The troops are not trained for march, offensive and defensive combat
3. Poor knowledge of the weapons and vehicles prevent effective usage
4. Servicemen have poor skills of acting as part of the unit or as single
5. Drivers have poor skills of driving the armoured vehicles
6. The gunners of tanks and BMP showed poor skills of fire at the moving targets, also getting confused in dynamic environment
7. Servicemen are not trained to provide medical aid and cannot use anti-shock medications
8. The units are not trained to perform a concentrated fire with the shift to another target
9. Servicemen are not skilled in techniques of moving over the battlefield
10. NCOs and Squadron Leaders are not trained to replace the officers on the battlefield.

The 'show of the absurd' continued.

13
APPROACHING GROZNY

On 22 December, elements of 104th Division started to move south towards Argun, to cut the R306 Highway, take positions towards the Argun River and destroy the bridges to prevent Dudaev's forces bringing reinforcements to Grozny from this direction. Another task was to prepare the move to take over Khankala airfield which in future, served as a supply base for Russian forces. Despite all the measures developed by General Rokhlin, together with 104th Division Commander, General Vadim Orlov, it looked like the Chechens were waiting for the Russians and prepared several ambush sites. Some of them were destroyed by artillery and airstrikes but others remained.

Fight Around Bekat-Yurt
The first to engage was the airborne company of 328th Regiment, moving over the fields aside from the highway, and managed to take positions east of Berkat-Yurt, towards Tsentora-Yurt and the railway bridge. It seemed that the appearance of the paratroopers from that direction was unexpected but very soon, reinforcements arrived, including a group of about 20 men, commanded by Usman Imaev, some men from Shali (it is not clear if it was one of the Shali units or just locals) and a group of Shamil Basaev RDB. Umaev offered to ambush the leading convoy but Basaev opposed, saying this would be too risky as Russians moved over the open fields. Umaev decided to perform the attack anyway, positioning his men along the railway tracks, rightfully thinking the Russians would not move over the bridge that had been extensively mined.

The convoy of the 238th Regiment was assembled in the shape of a 'U' with tanks and Tunguska SPAA guarding the front and flanks, while the main body of paratroopers had BMD and BTR-D. In total, there were about 40 vehicles that started to cross the railway. The Chechens were split in groups of two, each having RPG with 2–3 rounds. The idea was to make at least two shots, hopefully three, and retreat. When the first rounds fired at the rear section of the convoy, at about 00:15, Russians began to illuminate the area with flares returning heavy fire. Russian accounts state there were also tanks and howitzers but this remains uncertain.

Despite the sudden attack on the convoy and suffering losses, the elements of 238th Regiment were not taken unguarded. Concentrated fire kept the Chechens head-down, while the Russians took positions over an area of about 200–300m wide and 200m south of the railway tracks. Remaining on the edge of the RPG effective range, Chechens started to pull back while many were gunned down or wounded, including Usman Imaev, who was shot in the chest and received shrapnel in the back. Many of the Chechen vehicles

Russian BM-27 Uragan MLRS pictured near Grozny on 22 December 1994. Note the lack of tactical signs. (Photo by by Sergei Vilichkin)

2S3 Akatsiya, 152mm SPA in the Russian convoy sharing the road with local traffic near Sleptovskoe settlement on 22 December 1994. (Photo by Sergei Karpukhin)

truck full of explosives and detonate it on the bridge. The truck reached the centre of the bridge but for some reason, did not explode until commander of the flame-throwing platoon, Lieutenant Rim Magasumov, closed to the bridge and fired the RPO-A Shmel that successfully detonated the truck, demolishing one section of the bridge. In order to retreat from the site, Russians used a smokescreen. Taking over the area, Russians secured positions over the R306 Highway and towards Khankala. By 25 December, the Group positions were held by 129th MRR with 133rd OTB (west), Battalion of 337th Airborne Regiment (centre-south) and Battalion of 328th Airborne Regiment (east).

Change in Command

On 25 December, General Anatoly Kvashnin ordered preliminary preparations for entering Grozny and re-structured the Joint Group into four sub-groups as following:

Group North (CO General Konstantin Pulikovsky)

- 1/131st Brigade and 2/81st Regiment, located on the Terk Ridge north of Sadovoe
- 2/131st Brigade and 1/81st Regiment, located 5km north of Alkhan-Churt
- 276th Motor-Rifle Regiment, located on the Terk Ridge, in the area 6–7km north-east of Sadovoe

The Group included about 4,000 men, 80 tanks, over 200 APCs, and 60 artillery pieces.[1]

parked near the bridge were ignited by tanks and the evacuation of wounded became almost impossible. However, some managed to leave the area in private cars, whilst others went on foot.

During the night fight, Russians lost eight men killed and 19 wounded, two BMD destroyed and several disabled, three tanks disabled. Chechen losses cannot be estimated, with Russian accounting for at least 50 dead but the number was exaggerated as there were hardly 50 men who took part in the attack – some had decided not to challenge fate and returned to their villages.

The next day, Rokhlin ordered to destroy the bridge over the Argun River. The sappers could not approach the bridge due to heavy fire from the side of Argun, so it was decided to take a Ural

Group North-East (CO General Lev Rokhlin)

- 255th Motor-Rifle Regiment (two battalions)
- 33rd Motor-Rifle Regiment (two battalions)
- 68th Separate Reconnaissance Battalion
- 106th Separate Engineer-Sapper Battalion (m/u 73420)
- 173rd Separate Special Forces Battalion (OOSpN)
- 20th Separate Tank Battalion

All of the units were located around Tolstoi-Yurt and Pervomaiskaya. The Group included about 2,500 men, 30 tanks, 150 APCs and 30 artillery pieces.

Russian convoy of Internal troops lead by the T-72A tank of 141st Separate Tank Battalion spotted west of Samashki on 13 December 1994. (Photo by Georges DeKeerle)

Group East (CO General Nikolai Stas'kov)

- 129th Motor-Rifle Regiment (two motor-rifle battalions), located at Khankala
- 133rd Separate Tank Battalion, located at Khankala
- Joint regiment of 104th Airborne Division (two battalions), located west of Argun
- Joint battalion of 98th Airborne Division, located west of Argun

The Group included about 3,000 men, 40 tanks, 170 APCs and 40 artillery pieces.

Group West (CO General Valery Petruk)

Chechen locals inspect an unexploded FAB-250M-54 bomb after a Russian airstrike in Argun town, some 9km from Grozny, on 24 December 1994. The majority of such 'findings' were used as high-yield IEDs against Russian armour. (Photo by Alexander Zemlianichenko)

- 693rd Motor-Rifle Regiment, located near Oktyabr'skoe
- 503rd Motor-Rifle Regiment[2]
- 108th Separate Reconnaissance Battalion
- 141st Separate Tank Battalion
- Joint battalion of 21st Airborne Brigade
- Joint battalion of 56th Airborne Brigade
- Joint regiment of 76th Airborne Division (3 airborne battalions, 1 artillery battalion and reconnaissance company)
- Joint regiment of 106th Airborne Division (3 airborne battalions, 1 artillery battalion and reconnaissance company)

All units located between Oktyabr'skoe and some 1–2km southwest of Katayama District of Grozny.

The Group included about 5,000 men, 40 tanks, 300 APCs and 70 artillery pieces.

With all these arrangements mainly concerning only top commanders, there was no clear understanding of what type of combat the units would face. It was still largely believed that even when entering the city, there would be little, if any, opposition due to the factor of surprise and superiority.

Fight for Khankala

The newly arrived units of the Leningrad Military District – 129th Guards Motor-Rifle Regiment and 133rd Guards Separate Tank Battalion – were probably the most potent addition to General Rokhlin's Group. The two elements of 45th Guards Motor-Rifle 'Peacekeeping' Division were oriented on operations in conflict

T-80BV/B tanks of 3rd Company (CO Vladimir Voblikov), 133rd Guards Separate Tank Battalion, pictured riding east to Grozny on 26 December 1994. The first two tanks are T-80BV, the third is T-80B '551' of 1st Platoon Lead, Dmitry Zevakin. (via Efim Sandler)

zones as part of a multinational peacekeeping force. Both units were home-based in the same location – Village of Kamenka, Leningrad Oblast, and were very familiar with each other. Arriving in Mozdok in early December, the units had a chance to spend about a week for joint training and coordination. 129th Regiment, commanded by Colonel Borisov, had 1,690 men and 70 BTR-70s in two battalions –1st and 2nd. The 133rd Battalion, commanded by Lieutenant-Colonel Igor Turchenyuk, included 250 men, 120 tankers on 36 T-80BV, three T-80B and a T-80K, organised in three companies – 1st, 2nd and 3rd. All tanks were equipped with ERA blocks including explosive elements.

Chechen tankmen taking care of T-72B. Maintenance was not the strongest part of Chechen tankmen and only essential tasks were taken care of, resulting in most of the hardware falling into poor condition relatively quickly. (Photo by Mariusz Forecki)

On 24 December, the units received an order to move from Mozdok to Khankala and take it over. The assault detachment included 1st Motor-Rifle Battalion (CO Yuri Saulyak) on BTRs, and 1st Tank Company of T-80BV, of Captain Sergey Kachkovsky. The next day, the detachment marched towards Khankala and took it over without opposition (both settlement and airfield) – it looked like the Chechens had abandoned it. Some three hours later, the order was received to move 1.5km to the south and block the Grozny-Argun road.

On the night of 26 December, the Chechens attacked positions of the Russians and managed to destroy BTR-70, killing its commander and wounding several soldiers. The Russians returned fire, claiming several Chechens killed. During the same night, the Chechen battalion, Borz of Umalt Dashaev, probably supported by locals, arrived at Khankala previously vacated by Russians and started to prepare positions supported by tanks, BTRs and BM-21.

On 27 December, Russian forces were re-routed back to Khankala which was already occupied by Chechens. Both sides spent the day in preparations and sporadic artillery duels. On the next day, Russians started the assault with all elements of 129th Regiment and 133rd Battalion moving in the line from south to north with 1st Battalion from the left and 2nd from the right. At this point, Russians suffered their first loss; T-80BV No. 521 performed a sharp turn and fell from the slope attracting a lot of Chechen fire. Evacuating from the tank, the gunner was killed and two other crew members wounded. The Russian advance stuck and Chechens managed to knockout the MT-LBu command vehicle of artillery battery, killing its commander

An image showing a destroyed Chechen T-72A, reportedly taken after the fight for Khankala. The exact details of Chechen tank losses are almost impossible to trace as the tanks were of the same type and had no other markings besides white/blue/grey painted turrets. (via Efim Sandler)

On the other side, the 2nd and 3rd Tank Companies attacked Chechen positions along the airfield and the aviation compound. The T-80BV No. 536 tank of 2nd Company was hit by ATGM that detonated the ammunition, killing the tank commander. Two other crew members were wounded but managed to escape. Another T-80BV of the Company Commander, Lieutenant Zevakin, was hit by RPG but remained in working condition. Together with infantry of 2nd Battalion, the Russians managed to squeeze the Chechens out of the airfield and village but still were under incoming fire from the aviation compound. During the fire exchange Chechens lost their commander – Umalt Dashaev.[3]

On the next day, the elements of 98th Airborne Division approached Khankala and outflanked Chechen positions in the military compound from the right, facing the bridge to Grozny, preparing for assault. During the night, Chechens left their positions and fled to Grozny leaving all their armour and vehicles. In total, there were six Chechen tanks – five T-72A and one T-62. Russian losses included nine KIA (seven from 129th Regiment and two from 133rd Battalion) and 18 WIA (13 from 129th Regiment and five from 133rd Battalion). Another two were killed and four wounded when 1V119 Reostat (No. 197) of 217th Airborne Regiment, 98th Airborne Division, moved off the road and was destroyed by IED.

The armour losses included two T-80BV tanks that were completely destroyed (No. 517 and No. 536), the tank that fell (No. 521) was recovered several days later, another tank of 2nd Tank Company (probably No. 532) got its main gun stuck in the ground and fired, cutting off the barrel. Although not destroyed, it was never fully repaired and was used as a recovery vehicle instead. Two BTRs and one MT-LBu were also hit and destroyed. The fight for Khankala was a major and only armoured engagement of the whole campaign.

Messing Around Oktyabr'skoe

On the 28 December, the battalion of 234th Airborne Regiment, commanded by Lieutenant-Colonel Aleksander Iskrenko, reinforced by 165th Separate Reconnaissance Company of Senior Lieutenant Andrey Shevelev, was tasked with taking over three hills between Oktyabr'skoe and Alkhan-Kala, blocking the routes of possible Chechen reinforcements towards Grozny via Oktyabr'skoe, and later to take it over, supported by Divisional forces. It is not clear whether the paratroopers had any kind of intelligence on the enemy defences, but just before the operation, two companies of the battalion were routed to different tasks, leaving only one reduced company of 52 men with BMD, BTRD-Z and two GAZ-66 trucks, supported by one T-72A tank of 141st Separate Tank Battalion (TC – Lieutenant Nikolai Rostovsky).

According to Russian reports, the convoy was blocked by locals and had to move over the longer route exposed to the fire from Oktyabr'skoe. When the vehicles climbed the hill, one of the

T-80BV No 521 of 133rd Separate Tank Battalion that fell over the edge during the fight for Khankala on 28 December 1994. The tank was recovered several days later. (via Efim Sandler)

and a vehicle driver, and another T-80BV No. 517 – later destroyed by friendly fire to prevent capture.

In return, 1st Tank Company Commander, Captain Kachkovsky, scored one Chechen T-72A. Despite heavy anti-tank fire, the Russian tanks managed to give a good cover for infantry and scored another Chechen T-72A.

BMDs hit a mine and at the same time, a Chechen D-30 opened fire, almost instantly hitting the GAZ truck and killing all inside. The second GAZ was also hit but fortunately for the Russians, the round travelled between the cabin and the trunk and exploded at a safe distance.

The Russians found themselves under heavy fire and lost about half their force – killed or wounded. Despite requests for artillery and air support, nothing arrived. The senior officer of the Russian force, Head of Battalion HQ, Major Vladimir Kolybabinsky – an experienced Afghan War veteran – quickly regrouped his men and decided to perform a concentrated attack using the force from one platoon, under the cover of BTRD-Z and T-72 tank. On the other side of the route, the members of 165th Company deployed ATGMs and covered the attack, knocking out several targets. The tank commander, Lieutenant Rostovsky, led the attack but coming close to the Chechen lines, suddenly moved backwards – one version says it was hit or developed a malfunction in the main gun, another suggests the gunner was a new soldier and did not know how to fire, thus, they switched places. Soon, the tank re-joined the battle and destroyed the Chechen BMP but was hit by ATGM that killed Lieutenant Rostovsky and wounded the rest of the crew (the driver later died from his wounds).

Meanwhile, the paratroopers managed to take over the Chechen positions and capture one D-30 and a tank or BMP, with a Utyos NSV heavy machine gun that was used against the Chechens. The Reconnaissance Company came under attack from about 100 men coming from Grozny on KamAZ tracks, supported by a couple of armour pieces. With only 30 men on five BMDs, Lieutenant Shevelev managed to outmanoeuvre the Chechens and set-up his unit on superior positions, repulsed the attack with one killed and several wounded, including himself. The Russian losses were 18 men, 16 of them killed in a GAZ truck hit by D-30. Chechen losses estimated about 20–30 men.[4]

On 30 December, Oktyabr'skoe was secured by the elements of 76th Airborne Division. However, the skirmishes with Chechens continued on a small scale, claiming men and materiel from both sides. The numbers are not known but both sides reported 'hundreds of enemies' killed with only minimal losses for their own. These fake reports haunted the whole campaign from the start to the end. In addition, Russians continued losing men and machines due to non-combat related accidents like careless operation of weapons or technical ignorance. For example, the T-80BV tank of 133rd Battalion was destroyed by fire due to the lack of the engine thermal shield that the crew forgot to re-install after maintenance.

14
MOVING INTO THE CITY (30–31 DECEMBER 1994)

The decision to push into Grozny was probably the most important and controversial of the whole campaign. On the afternoon of 26 December, the Russian Minister of Defence, Pavel Grachev, held a meeting in his railway command post in Mozdok. The main question was the possibility of a special operation to take over Dzhokhar Dudaev's command compartment in the President's Palace, in the centre of Grozny, by the Special Forces joint command. The meeting was attended by the Minister of Interior, Victor Erin, Head of Counter-Intelligence, Sergey Stepashin, Deputy Head of GRU, Valentin Korabelnikov, Head of FSB Anti-Terror Centre HQ, Dmitry Gerasimov, FSB 'Alfa' Group Commander, Gennady Zaitsev and several other top officers of FSO, FSB and the Ministry of Defence.

The report on the situation in Grozny was given by the Chief Intelligence Officer of Airborne Corps, Colonel Pavel Popovskikh. The information gathered via all available means, showed a clear picture of the defensive positions, weapons and the projected amount of Chechen units that were estimated at 2,000–2,500 militants (in fact, this proved to be quite precise in regard to regular units although there were more Chechen troops in Grozny when territorial defences and local armed groups were considered).

In response, Russian forces could commit no more than 600 Special Forces of various units while the Minister of Interior, Victor Erin, rejected the participation of his troops. By the end of the meeting, Pavel Grachev summarised, 'We will not assault Grozny. In the middle of January, we will start to squeeze them out of the city. Let them run into [the] mountains, there we kill them in spring.'

Chechen territorial defences (aka local volunteers) pictured west of Grozny on 17 December 1994. These militants improvised their equipment and weapons and did not excel in discipline, often leaving the battlefield for home. (Photo by Alexander Zemlianichenko)

The next day, Grachev, Erin and Stepashin, flew to Moscow. They were back on the same day with orders to put troops into Grozny. Whether the decision was made by President Yeltsin personally, or by a group of people close to him – is unknown, but Pavel Grachev, knowing the situation military-wise, did not oppose it and gave it a green light. Pavel Grachev proved many things – being incompetent in military affairs was not one of them. On the other hand, he was not once accused of lacking the civilian courage to confront his political superiors. However, he was back in Mozdok by the end of 27 December 1994 with the orders to take over Grozny by 1 January 1995.[1]

T-80VB tank of 6th Guards Tank Regiment reporting to 81st Guards Motor-Rifle Regiment, 90th Guards Tank Division, pictured departing the homebase near the town of Chebarkul, on 13 December to reinforce the Russian forces in Chechnya. (Efim Sandler collection)

The planning of the operation took the whole of 28 December and the orders to the units were only issued on the next day. For example, Commander of the Group North, Konstantin Pulikovsky, on the morning of 29 December, announced that no-one would enter the city until the Group was fully trained, divided into assault detachments, et cetera. He was then called to Mozdok and returned on 30 December, with orders to move towards the initial positions and to be ready for assault.

The same situation was in Group East; General Nikolai Stas'kov received the orders having less than 48 hours to work out the operation details with all his units. For example, starting with the coordination with artillery, it appeared to be that majority of crews had never fired a round and could not operate using the maps. The maps provided by the topography service were of different types – some from 1972, others from 1983 or 1985 at the best. None of the maps considered the developments of the recent years, even street names had not been updated. Many platoon and company commanders received only Xerox copies in such bad quality they could barely read the names of the streets, or they just received schematic plans copied by hand. It appeared there were not enough maps and instead, there were hand-drawn plans of the routes. Support units, like anti-aircraft artillery and engineers, did not received maps at all – they were told to follow their parent unit armour. On the day of 30 December, the unit commanders performed briefs on the mock-up models and theoretical trainings without armour, that de facto, proved to be another absurdity under the circumstances.

The Plan

The plan to take over Grozny was developed by the General Operational Directorate, Generals Kvashnin, Shevtsov, Baryn'kin and others, under the supervision of the Head of General HQ, General Mikhail Kolesnikov. The major objectives were the President's Palace, government (Sovmin), TV, radio and the railway station. The idea was to move the troops from three directions and in cooperation with Ministry of Interior and FSB, secure the centre of the city and Katayama District.

It seems that Russian Military Command did not believe in any kind of serious opposition but just in case, ordered to have several assault detachments; motor-rifle or paratrooper battalion (reduced) with attached tank companies and additional assets. The detachments had a very large number of armoured vehicles compared to the available infantry and probably, the idea was to scare the Chechens. The troops were not supposed to open fire or sweep residential buildings without any serious reason but were to focus on blocking the administrative buildings.

From the Group North, the two detachments of 81st MRR were moving on the right flank, while the detachment of 25th5 MRR (Group North-East) was planned to move from the left flank and secure the northern side, including the city centre on the western bank of the Sunzha River with the President's Palace and government building, from the north. 131st Brigade was tasked to provide the corridor and secure the rear limited by the Neftyanka River. Two detachments of Group West were tasked to secure railway station and block the government buildings from the south. Katayama District was the responsibility of joint detachments of 106th and 76th Airborne Divisions.

For the sake of deception, two detachments of 129th MRR and 98th Airborne Division (Group East) were supposed to simulate the major effort and advance along the railway tracks and take over the bridges blocking the centre of the city and thus, finalising a major part of the operation. The troops had no tasks to clean the Palace or other objectives but wait for the assault teams from the Ministry of Interior and FSB. The operation was supposed to last up to 10 hours, but an extended option was also considered in case of heavy opposition.[2]

Anatoly Kvashnin personally, one-by-one, called the commanders of the regiments and defined their tasks, drawing marks on the map by pencil and instantly erasing them.[3] Known for his negligence to details, Kvashnin was given only the most complex tasks, leaving the commanders to work out the rest. The result being that officers did not know who their neighbours were and had no idea of their plans. Moreover, their superior commanders had no clear idea of the assignments of their subordinate units. For example, LXVII

Corps Commander, General Pulikovsky, who commanded Group North, did not know the particular tasks of 81st Regiment and learned about them from Regiment CO, Aleksander Yaroslavtsev, during the Group brief on 30 December. The structure and order of assault detachments were defined by Anatoly Kvashnin and his team without any reasonable logic. The tanks were spread over the infantry battalions, while each platoon was supposed to have a tank leading the convoy. This organisation voided any ability of tank unit commanders to control their respective units, as there was no visible connection between the tanks.

Overall, there was a visible similarity with the events of October 1993, when the armoured convoys moving over the major streets of Moscow, blocked the Supreme Soviet building (White House) and after a short tank fire barrage, effectively forced the defenders to surrender. Some veterans also called it 'parade formation'.

Chechen Preparations

The exact amount of Grozny defenders is unknown but can be estimated from 1,500 to 3,000 of regular Chechen Armed Forces and about the same number of local volunteers, coming from or outside Grozny, bearing in mind that Grozny was never fully blocked. Thus, the overall numbers can vary from 3,000 to 6,000. There was a widespread opinion that the city was prepared for echeloned defences with three circles, but it looks that such idea may only exist in the mind of Ichrekia armed forces HQ Chief, Aslan Maskhadov, or his top commanders. The real idea of the Grozny defences was based on two very simple principles – mobility and coordination. Every regular unit had its own sector and supervised the local volunteers, basically telling them what to do. Every unit was split into numerous sub-units and down to groups of 5–10 people, often moving in private cars communicating via Motorola radios. The most potent units like RDB and Borz, were responsible for the areas along the possible routes of Russian advance and it was not difficult to figure out those, the Presidents Guard and DGB units were placed around their natural habitat – government buildings. Each unit was responsible for elaborating the plans and coordination between the groups and with other units. On the other hand, the groups could act completely independent without centralised command or join neighbouring forces if necessary.

Chechen preparations for the assault on Grozny were never a secret and a lot of media agencies showed how it was progressing – AP, Reuters, Russian NTV, et cetera. Unsurprisingly, Chechens utilised the government buildings for the toughest defences – the Soviet style structures of reinforced concrete could withstand heavy artillery and aviation bombardments. Another popular myth surrounds special suicide units, so-called Gazavat-warriors, that were trained to die but not to surrender – none of this existed in Chechnya. In the nature of the Armed Forces of Ichkeria, every member who sacrificed his life for the cause of Ichkeria, was considered Shaheed (or Martyr), and it was an honour to volunteer for such missions that might result in a death.

Another myth regards the scores of foreign mercenaries, including so-called 'white stockings' – professional female sharpshooters from Baltic states, trained as members of biathlon teams. At the beginning of hostilities, there was a very small amount of volunteers from several Muslim countries, mainly of Chechen origin, and some from Ukraine and possibly from Baltic states. There were no female snipers of any kind, in Chechen regular units at this stage, but some Chechen women volunteered to be medical assistants. For example, in his memories, Ruslan Gelaev mentioned that he was surprised to see two young girls in Grozny acting as nurses who also knew how to use the firearms.[4]

Another issue was the deployment of heavy weapons like tanks and artillery. The amount of tanks available for the defences of Grozny by 30 December 1994 was no more than 30 and practically, they were spread between the various units, which does not mean that all 30 tanks were in the city.[5] There was no common pattern of their usage and it mainly depended on the mindset of the unit commander – some used them as pillboxes, others planned to have them as mobile artillery. All tanks were painted in white or light blue – either whole or just turrets, and many were decorated with flags.

The artillery presented more or less, the same story but in most cases, it was planned to fire from fixed positions inside buildings or barns on the outskirts of Grozny. Artillery assets included D-30, MT-12 and even the old M-44. Most of the BM-21 MRLs inherited from the Russians were out of ammunition or destroyed and could not do much besides releasing the occasional salvo on incoming convoys. However, as it was on 30 December in Urus-Martan, a majority of cases missed their target or hit villages. Other heavy weapons included vehicle based 12.7mm Utes NSV and 23mm ZU-23-2 machine guns.

The statement 'every building is a fortress' mostly related to the super-structures of the government buildings, while the majority of residential houses were not treated as such. Fortifications included the preparation of the positions inside the buildings for snipers and anti-tank teams – utilising mostly lower and upper floors, mouse-holing the walls for rapid switching of positions both in horizontal and vertical directions. Along the roads leading into the city centre, positions were established to support direct artillery and tank fire.

There was also the preparation of numerous storage sites for supplies to include ammunitions, medications, food, et cetera, and the organisation of shelters and medical care in the fortified basements that were turned into bunkers. A certain amount of mining of possible routes of advance was also undertaken with numerous cases of mining the access of multi-story buildings, stairs and roofs.

Many sniper positions also include range cards. Positions in the basements kept the militants safe from Russian tank guns, the turrets of which were unable to depress their tubes sufficiently. Vaulted and sloped add-on roofs reduced the effects of a Russian RPO-A Shmel flamethrower and other systems. For example, on the route of VIII Army Corps along Petropavlovsk Highway, two brick factories with walls of about 1m thick, were prepared to hold numerous positions; behind the walls was a trench of about 1.5m deep, giving good options for switching positions. The junctions on the highway were mined with heavy IEDs.

Communications were paramount. Every group had short range portable radio devices of Western origin like Motorola and Alinco, while the Chechens commanders used satellite phones. During the early stage of the war, Russian EW never succeeded to disrupt or suppress Chechen communications as the latter did not utilise military systems. On the other hand, the Chechens used old Soviet equipment to break into Russian transmissions and created havoc. While the fact of an upcoming assault was obvious, the only information the Chechens did not know about, was timing. Nevertheless, the Russians promptly informed them by dropping leaflets over the city.

Eventually, the assault on New Year's Eve was as surprising to Chechens as it was for the Russians. It is important to state that a good portion of the regulars were sent out of Grozny as the Chechen leadership was pretty sober regarding the prospect of the Russians

Russian AGS-17 team in the trenches near Grozny, December 1994. Russian units preferred to camp in the open fields in order to minimise the threat of being attacked by the Chechens. In this situation, infantry heavy weapons like AGS, SPG and mortars could be exploited to perfect efficiency. (Photo by TASS)

T-72A '510' of 1st Company Commander, Yuri Schepin, of 131st OMSBr pictured on the Terk Ridge in late December 1994 (Photo by Vladimir Svartsevich)

taking the city sooner or later, having planned for partisan warfare in the long run.

Deployment to Initial Positions

Group North
131st Brigade
During the day on 30 December, 131st Brigade was busy with engineering arrangements for positions that were taken the previous day. All tank crews were tasked with practice runs and fire exercises. It seems this was rather a show-of-force than actual training. The Brigade was split into two detachments – first, one of 1st Motor-Rifle Battalion was tasked with securing the Rodina and Sadovoe settlements from the north, while the second of 2nd Battalion, followed the 81st MRR to reach the northern bank of Neftyanka River and secure the bridges. As a secondary task it was supposed to follow 81st MRR and secure the rear. In total, from 131st Brigade there were about 450 men in two motor-rifle battalions on BMP-2, tank battalion (reduced – about 25 T-72A tanks) and an anti-aircraft battery, as another battery went to 81st MRR. There were also additional units such as artillery, operating 2S1 Gvozdika but those were mostly left in the rear positions.[6] During the commander's brief on 30 December, 131st Brigade CO, Colonel Ivan Savin, once again updated on the tasks that were focused on holding positions on the left bank of Neftyanka River and Rodina Sovkhoz. By then, there were no plans to deploy 131st Brigade into Grozny.

81st Motor-Rifle Regiment
The 81st MRR moved towards its starting positions, some 2km north to the Grozny-Severny airport and was ready by 20:00. At the same time, all commanders were conducting the brief with the Group Commander, General Pulikovsky, to finalise the tasks and coordinate the actions. For the 81st Regiment, there were three major objectives – the airport (due by 10:00), Khmelnitsky-Mayakovskaya Junction (due by 16:00) and optional – 1st Battalion to take over the railway station and 2nd Battalion to block the President's Palace from the north-west. The regiment was reinforced by six 2K22 Tunguska SPAA of the anti-aircraft battalion of 131st Brigade with two TZM vehicles. Each battalion had two Tunguska, one was left with HQ Group and one with 33rd Separate Signalling Battalion (m/u 94015) of 90th Tank Division. The regiment received Obstacle Breeching Detachment (probably from 1st Guards Engineer-Sapper Brigade, m/u 11105) including 46 officers and soldiers, three BTR-80, four IMR-2 and three UR-77. Each battalion received also one BTR, one BREM and two pontoon vehicles (or AVLB bridge-layers) from the same Brigade, plus one R-145BM for communications of 33rd Signalling Battalion of 90th Division. Another two R-145BM were in the HQ Group. The forward element was Reconnaissance Company (CO Evgeny Kolomeitsev) which had only 34 men on five BRM-K and four BRDM-2. The whole party had probably about 500–600 men and about 100 pieces of armour.[7]

276th Motor-Rifle Regiment
The 276th Motor-Rifle Regiment (m/u 69771) of 34th Ordzhonikidze Simferopol Motor-Rifle Division of Ural Military District, based in Yekaterinburg, had completed its preparations by 20 December and left for Mozdok on 23 December. The Regiment, commanded by Colonel Sergey Bunin, included two motor-rifle battalions (1st and

Russian IMR-2 recovery vehicle working on the muddy ground under the cover of BMD-1 of Airborne Corps on 16 December 1994. Note that IMRs were never part of Airborne Corps units but operated by the Engineers assigned to the Group. (Photo by Georges DeKeerle)

2K22 Tunguska '606' and BMP-2 of 131st Separate Motor-Rifle Brigade near Grozny. The anti-aircraft battalion of the Brigade was split between the Brigade and 81st Regiment. (Photo by Vladimir Svartsevich)

was to move into Grozny over the Petropavlovsk Highway, after crossing the bridge over the Neftyanka River, to secure the left flank of the major effort (by Group North). General Rokhlin employed his contacts with the opposition and received information that the plan was compromised; the whole way over the Petropavlovsk Hwy contained sets of ambushes, including high-yield explosives under the road. Not being informed about moving into Grozny, General Lev Rokhlin started to develop his own plan of action and on 27 December, he conducted a commander's meeting to set-up the tasks in a very simple way. From the logbook of VIII Army Corps:

3rd), on BMP-1, tank battalion with T-72B1, artillery battalion with 2S1, mortar battery with 2S12, anti-aircraft battalion with ZSU-23-4, and support units. As usual, the men and materiel were picked up from the whole Military District. By 29 December, a Regiment of 1297 men, 73 BMPs, 31 tanks and 24 artillery pieces, was unloaded in Mozdok and by 05:00 moved towards Grozny to report to Group North. At about 19:00, Colonel Bunin received an order to replace 131st Brigade north of Sadovoe by 04:00, 31 December. By that time, the Regiment was on the Terk Ridge and reached its initial position at 06.30.

Group North-East

General Lev Rokhlin's Group was tasked to perform as backup for Group North and made some moves to secure the objectives on the way to President's Palace. Originally, the plan for Group North-East

13:00 – meeting with Corps Commander
General guidelines:
- Keep the men alive
- Accomplish the task. Need to be well-prepared. Check each and every soldier personally

The upcoming tasks:
1. Moving in parallel to Sunja River
2. Breach the corridor, find the route and move into the city centre while securing the flank of the Joint Group

The way of action:
1. Recon the places that they are not waiting for us
2. Perform artillery strikes at the anticipated positions of the enemy
3. Moving with three groups:

a. 255th MRR tasked to overcome about 2/3 of the route maintaining extensive fire.
b. 33rd MRR moving in the tail of 255th while taking over the tall buildings, blocking the route and setting the outposts. It is also tasked with taking control over the route and delivery of the supplies.
c. 6th8 ORB following the first party of 255th MRR, securing the flanks. Each officer should have the 1:50,000 map.

Issues to solve:
1. Blocking. Each bock has the number of assigned BTR and names of the team. Block commander knows the task.
2. Assign the tasks.
3. 33rd MRR has the same assault group structure as 255th MRR.
4. Who and when will be relieved from tasks.
5. Check the gear.
6. Mukha (RPG-18) – all should be trained and take live firings.
7. The readiness of BTR drivers – who will come and who will not.
8. BTRs should be full of ammunition (there was other choice of getting the ammunition to the front line).
9. Establish the armoured group for casualties' evacuation. Establish the radio contact.
10. Set-up observation posts along the route. Find the spots.

Command post in the centre of the forces. The artillery and reserve group stays in Tolstoi-Yurt.

The pathfinding job was performed by 173rd OOSpN (Special Forces Detachment, m/u 11879), commanded by Major Vladimir Nedobezhkin, which acted from 104th Airborne Divisional base near Berkat-Yurt, and 68th ORB (Separate Reconnaissance Battalion, m/u 23562) of 20th Motor-Rifle Division, commanded by Major Dmitry Grebenichenko, acting from the main Group base near Tolstoi-Yurt. Upon Rokhlin's orders, the groups located the three routes and mapped the relevant information. The observation mapping continued up until the morning of 31 December thus, Group Command had real-time data and situational awareness.

During the raid on 29 December, the Group of 173rd Detachment in the area of Berkat-Yurt, spotted a tank hidden in the Milk-Produce Farm (MTF), some 300m from the positions of Group East. During the short engagement, the tank was disabled by Russian T-72 fire but one officer of 68th ORB, taking part in the raid, was shot dead. On the next morning, the Russians returned to the Milk Farm reinforced by tanks and Tunguska SPAA. They found the Chechen tank still sitting on the same spot, a D-30 howitzer and a mortar with ammunition.

255th Motor-Rifle Regiment
The assault detachment was based on the 1st Motor-Rifle Battalion, followed by the armoured Group of 20th Separate Tank Battalion with 173rd Detachment and finally, 2nd Battalion.[8] The flanks were covered by 68th ORB. By 30 December, the element's assault detachment was located in the area south of Tolstoi-Yurt and Goryacheistochnenskaya. The engineering assets came from 109 Separate Engineering-Sapper Battalion (m/u 10885), relocated to Volgograd from East Germany in 1993 and commanded by Major Valery Rostovschikov. The combat order of the Regiment, commanded by Colonel Sergey Rudskoy, assigned for the assault included only 340 men with 63 officers, 28 BTRs, three BRDMs and three BRMs. The total number of the assault detachment was about 600–650 men whilst most of the artillery, support units and reserve group were left in Tolstoi-Yurt.

33rd Motor-Rifle Regiment
The 33rd Separate Berlin Don-Cossack Motor-Rifle Regiment (m/u 42746), commanded by Colonel Vladimir Vereschagin, was not part of the VIII Army Corps but reported directly to the North-Caucasian Military District. It arrived at the area of operations in late December and was assigned to simulate the move towards Petropavlovsk Hwy, whilst even the Regiment Commander has no idea it was a deception and the main effort would come north with 255th MRR. The Regiment was located east of Petropavlovskya. On the morning of 30 December, the forward elements of 1st Motor-Rifle Battalion took over the Neftyanka River bridge without opposition and started to make engineering arrangements – the bait was taken.

The Chechens began moving reinforcements towards the bridge and at about 16:00 started to barrage the Russians with mortar and small arms fire. At some point, Rokhlin ordered 33rd Regiment to pull back from the bridge but kept some elements to work on fake preparations for crossing. Once again, Rokhlin made up his mind when he ordered to hold, observe and pinpoint Chechen positions while the Chechens kept moving troops towards the bridge. During the night, the Russians performed a massive artillery strike on the

Commanders of 133rd Separate Tank Battalion pictured in Khankala on 30 December 1994. From left to right – Igor Turchenyuk (Battalion CO), Rinat Akhmedzyanov (Battalion Technical Officer), Dmitry Zevakin (2nd Company CO), Sergey Kisel (2nd Company XO), Sergey Kachkovsky (1st Company CO), Sergey Kurnosenko (Battalion HQ Officer). (via 133rd Battalion veterans).

mapped positions and 33rd Regiment pulled out towards its actual objectives.

Group East

The Group's major task was deception, aka simulating the main effort of attracting major forces of Chechens while the other groups would accomplish the tasks. Russian Command did not anticipate any significant resistance on this direction thus, the Group had probably the most comprehensive task – to enter the city from Khankala, moving fast via Minutka Square and blocking the government area from the East. Technically, the Group was responsible for the whole part of Grozny, east of Sunja River.

The original plan developed in Joint Group HQ was to move over the Khankalskaya St – Minutka Square – Lenin Parkway – President Palace, passing via Minutka Tunnel. However, General Stas'kov changed the plan to bypass the obvious trap and ordered to move over the Mikhail Kol'bus Street along the railways, then to take the turn north. The whole party was combined from two detachments – one of 129th MRR and another from joint battalion of 98th Airborne Division. The units of 104th Airborne Division stayed at the initial positions blocking Argun direction from the north.

129th MRR

The first task of the 129th Guards Motor-Rifle Regiment was to reach and secure Minutka Square. The first assault detachment was assembled with 1st Motor-Rifle Battalion of Major Saulyak (BTR-70) with 1st Tank Company (CO Captain Kachkovsky) of 133rd Guards Separate Tank Battalion, a battery of ZSU-23-4M (five pieces) followed by reduced motor-rifle battalion (actually, one company on BTR-70), commanded by Battalion CO, Major Goncharuk, with a tank company with Lieutenant Sergey Kisel.9

The second convoy was led by the reconnaissance platoon of 129th Regiment on BRM, tanks of 133rd Battalion (probably 3rd Company), the 7th Company of 217th Airborne Regiment on 6 BMD-1, elements of 98th Division reconnaissance, several Ural trucks, probably towing D-30 howitzers, two 2S9 Nona SPA and some command vehicles. The closing force was 8th Company of 217th Airborne Regiment on six BMD-1 with Battalion HQ and a BRM.[10] The 2nd Motor-Rifle Company of 129th Regiment was not included in the convoy and remained to secure the Grozny-Argun road, supported by a tank platoon of 3rd Company, 133rd Battalion. The artillery battalion operating 2S1, support elements of 129th Regiment, were left in Khankala, as well as 9th Company of 217th Airborne Regiment that replaced 129th Regiment elements. None of the detachments included any kind of engineering support besides the vehicles of 129th Regiment, if any.

Group West
693 MRR

The Group commanded by XLII Army Corps XO, General Valery Petruk, was tasked with moving into Grozny from west and south-west by two assault detachments, combined from the elements of 693rd MRR (CO Colonel Vasily Prizemlin) and 239th Separate Reconnaissance Battalion (m/u 12356) of 19th Motor-Rifle Division. The detachments were to move over Industrialnaya St. and split into two directions – one of the 1st Motor-Rifle Battalion shifting left over Popovicha St. reaching the railway station and moving north, towards the city market, Rosa Luxembourg St. and from there, to block the President's Palace from the west.

The second detachment was ordered to secure the area between the Sunja River and the railway hub, securing the railway station

Defenders of Grozny pictured on 30 December 1994. These are the members of one of the regular units of the Armed Forces of Ichkeria recognisable by their weapon sets but still wearing all kinds of apparel. (Photo by Alexander Zemlanichenko)

and facilities around. In another version. the second detachment moved in the tail of the first one as there was no precise planning and no maps provided. The communications were loose and no-one had any idea of the neighbouring units. At least on paper, the order of 693rd Regiment stood at 1,737 men, 19 tanks, 35 BMPs, 32 BTRs, and 32 artillery pieces.[11] In reality, the force entering Grozny did not count more than 700 men, the tank battalion, commanded by Captain Yuri Sulemenko was split between the elements of the Group with no centralised management. It is not clear if there was any kind of engineering support and what other units took part in the operation reporting to 19th MRD. On 30 December, the units were positioned between Oltyabr'skoe and Stary Poselok. The overall supervision for the detachments was managed by 19th MRD CO, Colonel Gennady Kandalin.

76th Airborne Division

The Joint Detachment of 76th Guards Chernigov Airborne Division (m/u 07264 based in Pskov), commanded by General Ivan Babichev included the following elements:

- Joint Battalion of 104th Airborne Regiment (m/u 32515) commanded by Lieutenant-Colonel Sergey Tulin
- Joint Battalion of 234th Airborne Regiment (m/u 74268) commanded by Lieutenant-Colonel Alexander Iskrenko

Iconic image taken at Minutka Square just before the launch of the Russian assault – the deserted city with lone civilians trying to flee, under the huge poster in Ichkeria colors, saying 'FREEDOM' (Photo by Igor Mikhalev)

- Joint Battalion of 237th Airborne Regiment (m/u 57264) commanded by Lieutenant-Colonel Vyacheslav Sivko
- SPA Battalion of 1140th Artillery Regiment (m/u 45277) commanded by Colonel Anatoly Kireev
- 51st Separate Reconnaissance Company (m/u 64004) commanded by Senior Lieutenant Andrey Shevelev
- Joint Battalion of 21st Separate Airborne Brigade (m/u 54801) commanded by Colonel Valentin Mar'in
- Joint Battalion of 56th Separate Airborne Brigade (m/u 74507) commanded by Lieutenant-Colonel Alexander Sotnik
- Tank Company (reduced – six tanks) of 693rd MRR

The units were positioned around Oktyabr'skoe and tasked with moving over the Andreev Valley and the road to Grozny (Dorozhnaya St.) to secure the Zavodskoy District and backup the major assault force of 19th MRD. It is not clear how many troops took part in the assault but on paper, by the start of operation, there were about 1,700 men from different units. The combat order that entered Grozny was much less.

106th Guards Tula Airborne Assault Division

The Joint Detachment of 106th VDV Division (m/u 55599) commanded by Colonel Stanislav Semenyuta included the following elements:

- Joint Battalion of 51st VDV Regiment (m/u 33842) commanded by Lieutenant-Colonel Vladimir Krymsky.
- Joint Battalion of 137th VDV Regiment (m/u 41450) commanded by Lieutenant-Colonel Gleb Yurchenko.
- SPA Battalion of 1182nd Artillery Regiment (m/u 93723) commanded by Major Alexander Silin.
- Tank Company (reduced – seven tanks) of 693rd MRR.

The 106th VDV Division was the most northern element of the Group, positioned south-west of Tashkala at the southern outskirts of Katayama District.

BIBLIOGRAPHY

Akhmadov Ilyas, Lanskoy Miriam. *The Chechen Struggle. Independence Won and Lost* (New York: PALGRAVE MACMILLAN, 2010)

Akhmadov Yavus, *Chechen History from the Ancient Times to the End of XVIII Century* (Mir Tvoemu Domu Publishing, 2001)

Akhmadov Yavus, Khasmagomadov Edil'bek. *Chechen History in XIX-XX Centuries* (Puls Publishing House, 2005)

Alero Isa. *Wolfs' Time. The Notes of Chechen War Soldier.* Soldier of Fortune Magazine 4–7, 1997. Moscow

Alyokhin Gennady. *The Breakdown of Unannounced War. First Chechen.* Military Memoirs (Veche), 2020

Antipov Andrey. *Lev Rokhlin. The Life and Death of a General.* EKSM Press, Moscow. 1998

Astashkin Nikolai. *On the Wolfs' Track. Chechen Wars Chronicles.* Veche Publishing House. Moscow 2005.

Asuev Sherip. *It was like that.* Chronicles of 1988–1993. Grozny, 1993

Bataeva R. *The Way to the Victory.* Commendation letters of Chechens during Great Patriotic War. Directorate of Archive of the Government of Chechen Republic, 2015

Belogrud Vladislav. *Tanks in the Fights for Grozny, Part 1.* Frontline Illustration Periodic. Strategy KM Publishing. 9-2007, Moscow.

Belogrud Vladislav. *Tanks in the Fights for Grozny, Part 2.* Frontline Illustration Periodic. Strategy KM Publishing. 1-2008, Moscow.

Benedetti Francesco. *Freedom or Death. History of the Chechen Republic of Ichkeria.* Volume one. From the Revolution to the First Chechen War (1991–1994). Independent publication. 2021

Billingsley Dodge. *Fangs of the Lone Wolf. Chechen Tactics in the Russian-Chechen Wars 1994–2009.* Helion & Company, Warwick, England, 2022.

Chentsov A. *Special Operation to Disarm Population of North-Caucasian Republics in 1925–1926.* Military University Reporter. 2009

Cherkasov Alexander, Trusevich Olga. *Unknown Soldier of Caucasian War. 1994–1996.* Memorial Human Rights Defence Centre Publishing. Moscow, 1997.

Collection of Decrees of President of Chechen Republic. From 1 November 1991 until 30 June 1992. Kniga Publishing House. Grozny, 1993.

Dadaev Yusup. *Shamils' Nadirs and Mudurs.* DINEM. Makhachkala, 2009

Donogo Khadzhi-Murad. *Shamils' Orders.* Shamil Foundation. Dagestan State Historical-Architectural Museum. Makhachkala, 1995

Efimov Mikhail. *Bomb for the Minister of Defence.* Soldier of Fortune Magazine. 7.2000. Moscow.

Efimov Mikhail. *Deceived and Slandered….* Soldier of Fortune Magazine. 12.2000. Moscow.

Galitsky Sergey. *In December of Ninety-Four. They Defended the Motherland.* Pirs Publishing House. Saint Petersburg. 2008

Galitsky Sergey. *The First Chechen War. They Defended the Motherland.* Galitsly S.G. Self-publishing. Saint Petersburg. 2020

Gantemirov Beslan. *Moscow Provided Dudaev with Weapons and Money.* Ogonyok Magazine No. 15 (4550). Moscow 1998

Gareev Ilshat. *Seventh Company.* Publishing Solutions. Ekaterinburg, 2018

Grodnensky Nikolay, *Non-ending War: The History of the Chechen Conflict.* Harvest, Minsk. 2004.

Karpov, Plotkin, *Armed Forces of Republic of Ichkeria. Uniform of Chechen Armed Forces Units.* Sergeant Magazine #2. Moscow, 1997

Kelimatov Akhmet. *Chechnya: In the Claws of Devil or On the Way to Self-Destruction.* ECOPRINT. Moscow. 2004

Khasbulatov Ruslan. *They did not let me to stop the war. The memories of peacekeeper.* Paleya. Moscow. 1995

Kiselyov Valery. *Nizhegorodians in Chechen War.* Self-publishing, Nizny Novgorod. 2000

Kislyi Yuri. *Everybody was shooting there …* Bratishka Magazine. 12.2001. Moscow

Knezys Stasis, Sedlickas Romanas. *The War in Chechnya.* Eastern European Studies. Texas University Press, 1999.

Kogan-Yasny Victor. *Chechen crossways. Articles, essays and documents.* Moscow. 1995

Kondrat'ev Vyacheslav. *Formidable Sky over Chechnya.* Kryl'ya Rodiny Magazine, 1996

Korshunov Oleg. *Black Snow of Grozny.* Bratishka Magazine Publishing, 2020

Kozlov Sergey. *Spetznaz GRU. Historical Encyclopaedia. Vol.4 Timelessness.* Russian Panorama Publishing House. Moscow. 2010

Kuleba Miroslaw. *Empire on the Knees.* Warsaw, 1998. Poland

Kuleba Miroslaw. *Shamil Basaev.* Odysseum, 2007. Poland

Kulikov Anatoly. *Heavy Stars.* War and Peace Books, Moscow. 2002

Kulikov Anatoly, Lembik Sergey. *Chechen Knot. The Chronicles of Armed Conflict 1994–1996.* House of Pedagogics Publishing. Moscow, 2000.

Kushnerev V. *Soviet Military Aviation in the Caucuses During 'Cold War' Years.* Military Academic Journal. No. 2(10), 2016. Moscow

Litovkin Victor. *Execution of 131 Brigade.* Izvestia newspaper, 11.01.1995

Lyakhovsky Aleksander. *Obsessed with Freedom. The Secrets of Caucasian Wars.* DetectivPress, Moscow. 2006 pp296–306

'Miami' Andrey. *Opposition – 3rd Party in Chechen Conflict.* Soldier of Fortune Magazine. 6–7, 1996. Moscow.

Milyukov Pavel, Yauk Konstantin. *I am 'Kalibr-10'. Assault on Grozny. January 1995.* Rybinsk Publishing House. Rybinsk (Yaroslavl), 2010

Morozov Vladislav. *The Big Eyes of Fear. Chechen Aviation 1992–94.* M-Hobby Magazine, 2013

Mozhokhin Oleg. *Politburo and state security agencies. 100th Anniversary of VChK.* Collection of documents. Kuchkovo Pole Publishing House. Moscow, 2017

Norin Evgeny. *Chechen War, Volume I. 1994–1996.* Chornaya Sotnya Publishing. 2021

Novichkov, Snegovsky, Sokolov, Shvarev. *Armed Forces in Chechen Conflict. Analysis-Summary-Conclusions.* HOLVEG-INFOGLOB-TRIVOLA. Paris-Moscow, 1995

Nosov Vitaly. *Officer's Confession. The Stories of Chechen War.* Kovcheg Publishing House, Moscow, 2004.

Oliker Olga. *Russia's Chechen Wars 1994–2000: Lessons from Urban Combat.* RAND, 2001

Petrov Victor. *Shooting? This Means the New Year Came!* Interview with Colonel Alexander Yaroslavtsev. Samara Newspaper. 26.12.1995

Popovskih Pavel. *Military Actions in Chechnya. Lessons and Conclusions*. Slavyansky Mir Journal. 1997

Raschepkin Konstantin. *This Strange and Horrible War*. Bratishka Magazine. 06.1999. Moscow

Rozhkov A. *Electronic Warfare in Wars and Armed Conflicts*. Kaliningrad, 2006

Runov Valentin. *Purgatory of Chechen War*. EKSMO. Yauza, 2009

Sergeev Andrey. *When Signalman Was Rolling a Reel*. Soldier of Fortune Magazine. June 1997. Moscow

Shestopalov Sergey. *Moloch of Grozny*. Rybinsk Publishing House. Rybinsk, Yaroslavl. 2013

Sigauri Iless. *Essays on the History and State System of Chechens since the Ancient Times*. Russkaya Zhizn' Publishing House, 1997

Skuratov Yury. *Letter of Prosecutor-General to Chairman of State Duma, Gennadiy Seleznyov, upon the cases of mass losses of Russian servicemen in Chechnya*. 1997

Sukholessky Alexander and others. *Chechen War: Combat Operations.* Yauza, EKSMO. Moscow, 2009

Troshev Gennady. *My War. The Diary of Trench General*. Vagrius Publishing. Moscow, 2001

Tsekhanovitch Boris. *Common War* (Moscow, Litres/self-published, 2018)

Yakubovich Nikolai, *Unknown Yakovlev, 'Iron' Designer* (Yauza, EKSMO, 2018)

Yandarbiev Zelimkhan, *Battle for Freedom* (Lviv, self-published, 1996)

Zaretsky Yuri. *'Cross of Gallantry', Soldier of Fortune Magazine*. December 2004

Zhirokhov Mikhail, *Burning Skies. Combat Aviation in Chechen War* (Yauza, EKSMO, 2011)

Websites

42nd Guards Yevpatorian, Red Banner, Motor-Rifle Division web site (http://42msd.ru/)

Abrosimov Igor. *Caucasian Knot*. Internet book (https://proza.ru/avtor/igorjan&book=12#12). 2021

Awards of Imperial Russia (http://medalirus.ru/)

Aviation Photography Portal (https://russianplanes.net/)

Aviation Disasters and Incidents in Russia and USSR (http://www.airdisaster.ru/)

Cherkasov Alexander. *1st Chechen War publications*. Memorial Human Rights Defence Centre. 2004.

Firsov Yakov. *Removed from commanding the Group*. Internet publication (https://dzen.ru/a/Y5mbcmRW1zUrAct_) 2022.

Hatuev I., Sugaipova A. *The Heroic Feat of the Pilot of Dasha Akaev*. Chechen State University.

Likhoded Dmitry. *The Armour of SS 5th Tank Division 'Wiking'* (https://www.dishmodels.ru/gshow.htm?p=18280) 2019

Loktionov Yuri. Letter published on the forum Desantura.ru (https://desantura.ru/forum/forum19/topic8795)

General Potapov. *Report of Russian Forces actions during special operation in Chechnya, 1994–1996*

Vechkanov Igor. *New Year Carousel*. Second Edition. Internet publication (http://artofwar.ru/w/wechkanow_i_w/viv.shtml). 2011

Voronov Vladimir. *Assault that never happened*. Radio Svoboda website. 2014 (www.svoboda.org)

Voronov Vladimir. *Tanks in Grozny*. Radio Svoboda website. 2014 (www.svoboda.org)

Shachnew Denis. *Assault as it was seen by a tankman*. Internet publication (http://artofwar.ru/s/shachnew_d_m). 2011

Strategic Rocket Forces (RVSN) Handbook (https://rvsn.info/)

Tsyganok Anatoly. *10 Days the Cancelled the Peace.* Internet publication. (https://versia.ru/v-1991-godu-usmirit-chechnyu-mozhno-bylo-silami-specnaza). 2021

Yauk Konstantin, *Russian Troops moving into Chechnya*. Live Journal publications (http://botter.livejournal.com/). 2008

Zhirokhov Mikhail. *Russian Air Force in 1st Chechen War*. Internet publication (www.airwar.ru/)

Discussions on the Facebook Group – History of the Chechen Republic of Ichkeia

Russian Troops moving into Chechnya. Desantura.ru forum. (https://desantura.ru/forum)

81 Regiment moving into Grozny. Desantura.ru forum. (https://desantura.ru/forum)

Memorial Page. *Chechnya 1994–1996*. Internet publication (http://www.skywar.ru/ChechenyaPamyat.html)

Zhukov Sergey. *Unrecoverable losses of Russian Forces on Northern Caucuses in November-December 1994.* (http://samlib.ru/z/zhukow_sergej_aleksandrowich/)

Zhukov Sergey. *Assault on Grozny 31 December 1994–1 January 1995.* (http://samlib.ru/z/zhukow_sergej_aleksandrowich/)

Group North memorial and reconstruction website (memoriesnorth.narod.ru)

Videos

Aldamova Zareta. *Ali Matsaev – Chechen pilot*. Documentary. Chechen State Tele-Radio Company 'Grozny'. 2014

Arsnovsky Alexander. *War in Chechnya*. Documentary. Information Centre of Chechen Republic, 1996

Baranov Dmitry. *Voice from Chorus*. Documentary. MIR TV Company, 1995

Chechen Resistance Fighters – Before and After Assault on Grozny. NIZAM Production, 2022

Illusion. *Dzhokhar Dudaev*. Documentary. ChGTRK Grozny. 2017

Keshishev Sergey. *Situation. Death for Loan*. ATV, 1995

Murad Mazaev. *14 Episodes, No Comments*. Chechen Films, 2004

Nevzorov Alexander. *Hell*. Alexander Nevzorov Production Centre, 1995

New Year Night of 81st Regiment. Documentary. 1995

Pobortsev Alexey. *On the Other Side of the War*. Documentary. NTV Channel, 2014. Moscow

Polunin Mikhail. *60 Hours of Maikop Brigade*. TV Company Seti NN, 1995

Prokopenko Igor. *Chechen Mantrap*. REN-TV, 2004

Sladkov Alexander. *26 November 1994 – First Assault, Unexpected*. RTR

Sladkov Alexander. *The Roadway to Hell*. Directorate of Informational and Society-Political Programmes, 1996

Sladkov Alexander. *Nameless Operation*. Directorate of Informational and Society-Political Programmes TV Vesti, 1999

Tankmen of Ichkeria. ZerkaloTV

Video footage of Russian and Chechen troops

Video footage from news channels: NTV, REN-TV, ORT, AP, Reuters, et cetera

NOTES

Chapter 1
1. The appearance of the ethnonym "Chechens" is usually associated with the name of the village of Chechen-aul, but the word "Chechen" itself has long been used as the name of the Chechen (Chachan) island in the Caspian Sea, right at the mouth of the Terek. It is also known about the existence of the city of Chechen (Chachan) and the Chechen River. A person called Murza Alkhan is named Chechen by Russian sources of the seventeenth century, in addition, the 'land of Chachan' is mentioned. But the word Chechen in relation to people, began to be used much later.

Chapter 2
1. Ivan Delpotzzo remained in captivity until 1804 when he was released for 8.400 Rubles paid by Prince Pavel Tsitsianov. For his sufferings, Delpotzzo had been called for duty, received the rank of Major-General and had been appointed Tsar Representative in Kabarda.

Chapter 3
1. Similar operations were conducted in Dagestan and Ingushetia. The unrest in Chechnya continued and peaked in 1929, 1932 and then in 1940, but all were aggressively suppressed by Soviet forces. The last political gang in Chechnya was officially eliminated in the 1950s.

Chapter 4
1. In Soviet Union the M3 tanks received respective designations M3l – 'light' for Stuart, and M3s – 'medium' for Lee.
2. In the Soviet and Russian sources this engagement near Sagopshin was called 'Caucasian Prokhorovka', and one that marked the end of the Mozdok-Malogbek Defensive Operation (also called Grozny Defensive Operation). Obviously, the battle near Sagopshin did not have any significant effect on the German offensive, though it remained one of the most successful engagements of the Soviet armoured units during the first part of the Second World War.

Chapter 5
1. Vladimir Komarov, two times Hero of Soviet Union – Soviet test pilot, Commander of Voskhod one spaceship that carried three cosmonauts launched in 1964, and Commander of Soyuz one spaceship launched in 1967 and ended up with disaster causing Komarov death.

Chapter 6
1. 9K52 Luna-M and 9K79 Tockha are ballistic missiles that can be armed with nuclear warheads A question stands regarding tactical nuclear weapons that reportedly were stored in the bases of Chechnya. As for now, there is no single trustworthy source but several loose opinions and accounts. Most likely is that all tactical warheads, if there were any, were dismantled and transferred to Russia before or during the first period of confrontation (Nov–Dec 1991).

Chapter 7
1. The unit was combined from former members of the Soviet armed forces who served in Afghanistan and had no connection to Afghan mujahedeen.
2. Officially, the 382nd Training Aviation Regiment with its assets, was transferred to Armavir College but, de facto in 1991, the latter was busy with absorbing the units withdrawing from Azerbaijan and the Regiment remained under the cap of Stavropol College.

Chapter 8
1. Along the opposition's version, heading over the Sultan Dudaev Bulevard, near Rossija movie-theatre, T-62 tank antenna touched the tram cables disabling all the equipment inside. The tank stuck, blocking the street and had to be abandoned and was set on fire. The only serious attack by Dudaev forces (probably RDB) was reportedly repulsed by concentred fire from BTRs and ZU-23-2. At about 02:00, the orders came to leave Grozny. By then, several BTRs had already developed engine issues and were towed by other vehicles which made every move very complicated. By the time of leaving, all the unserviceable armour and vehicles had been left behind.

Chapter 9
1. Ironically Dzhokhar Dudaev was one of the commanders of 1225th Heavy Bomber Aviation Regiment in 1980s.
2. This conversation has been reconstructed by reporters on basis of Grachev's interview.

Chapter 10
-

Chapter 11
-

Chapter 12
1. In his memoirs, General Rokhlin called Anatoly Kvashnin 'Energetic, kind and friendly person. Absolutely unprofessional in military affairs'.
2. For his actions Victor Ponomaryov was (posthumously) awarded the Title of Hero of Russian Federation by the Presidents' Decree No. 2254 of 31 December 1994.
3. Most probably, this was Deputy Commander of the Ground Forces, General Eduard Vorobyov.

Chapter 13
1. The reader should keep in mind that these numbers were 'paper only'. In reality, this and every other group of forces were managing their own road security, positions, supplies and other affairs. Moreover, it consisted of a much lower number of trained personnel and hardware ready for combat operations.
2. Although the majority of sources lists the 503: MRR as a part of the Group West at the time of the assault, this is entirely incorrect. The unit arrived from Vladikavkaz only at 15:00 on 1 January 1995. According to unconfirmed reports, the delay was caused by the regimental command intending to 'celebrate the New Year'.
3. A major loss for the Chechens was the death of Borz Special Forces Battalion Commander, Umalt Dashaev. Dashaev was one of the most potent commanders in Chechnya, joining the unit of Ruslan Shamaev just after it was established in 1991. Shamil Basaev considered Dashaev as the best man he ever served with: 'He was the only one who could share the load of responsibilities with me and take the command over the unit.' Later, after returning from Abkhazia, Dashaev received an offer from Ruslan Gelaev to join his newly established Special Forces Regiment as battalion commander. It is very possible that Dashaev would have evolved into one of Ichkeria's top military leaders of the same level as Basaev and Gelaev.
4. Lieutenant Andrey Shevelev of 165th Reconnaissance Company, was awarded a title of Hero of Russian Federation by Presidents' Decree of 27 January 1995. Lieutenant Nikolai Rostovsky of

141st Separate Tank Battalion, was awarded the title of Hero of Russian Federation (posthumously) by the President's Decree of 1 March 1995.

Chapter 14

1. The rumours of Grachev's birthday were obviously fake and were promoted sometime after the war by Gennady Troshev.
2. Although the majority of sources claims that the Russians were heavily dependent on the 'surprise factor', this is factually wrong: there could have been no surprise in a 10-hour combat operation in the same area.
3. According to the official version, the plan was presented to unit commanders on 25 December 1994, but it looks like it was shown to top commanders only.
4. All the rumours were invented by journalists on both sides and lately promoted by veterans, without any kind of details pointing at the fact that the rumours were unsubstantiated: not supported by any kind of hard evidence.
5. A careful analysis of the losses during the period of 31 December 1994 to 3 February 1995, revealed that 16 Chechen tanks were lost, most probably including those previously captured from Russian forces.
6. It remains unclear if the 131st Brigade included its own artillery element or deployed the Self-Propelled Artillery Battalion of 429th MRR, assigned to the 131st since 15 December 1994. During the assault on Grozny, two of its 1V15 vehicles were operating with 2nd Motor-Rifle Battalion
7. According to Regiment CO, Colonel Yaroslavtsev he had two combat battalions with 250 men each, minus mortar batteries and supply platoons, leaving just 160–170 men– the BMPs were crewed by 3–5 men leaving barely any infantry available for sweeping. Many soldiers of the Regiment were new recruits with no skills thus they were left behind.
8. Unlike Group North, Rokhlin kept the company sized armour element together, giving its commander, Major Rafikov, total control over the unit.
9. Sergey Kisel was a newly appointed commander replacing Lieutenant Zevakin who was wounded in Khankala. In order to assist Lieutenant Kisel, Battalion CO ordered Head of Battalion HQ, Captain Sergey Kurnosenko, to take place of a gunner in Company Commander T-80BV turret number 523.
10. According to memories of the veterans, there was no predefined structure of the convoy and the vehicles took whatever spot in the line. As the second convoy has been combined from various units, there were no communication between them.
11. As many other units, 693rd MRR was staffed and equipped according to the 'peace-time schedule' and had to be reinforced by men and materiel from other regiments. Eventually, being originally equipped with BMP-2, it received a battalion sized reinforcement of 503rd MRR (two motor-rifle companies) that operated BTR-80. It was the same with the tank battalion that had one original 693rd MRR Company of T-72B1, one company of 141st Separate Tank Battalion with T-72A and one company of 503rd MRR with T-72B1.

ABOUT THE AUTHOR

Born in the Union of Soviet Socialist Republics, Efim Sandler is a combat veteran of the Israeli Defence Force Armoured Corps and is currently living in the USA. An enthusiastic historian since his youth, he developed a deep interest in the armoured warfare of the Arab Israeli Wars and conflicts in the former USSR and has been collecting related information for decades. He is the co-author of the Lebanese Civil War series and after posting several articles about the Chechen Wars, this is his first book on the subject.